the
Mac OS X
conversion kit:

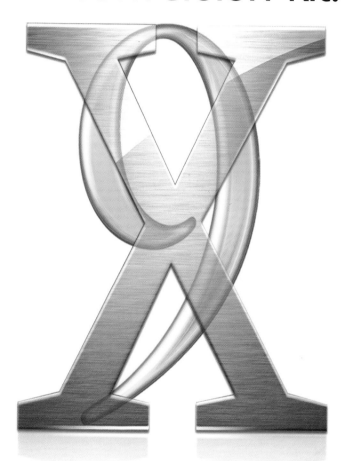

9 to 10 side by side

Scott Kelby

Mac OS X Conversion Kit

The Mac OS X
Conversion Kit Team

EDITOR
Richard Theriault

TECHNICAL EDITORS
Lesa Snider
Chris Main

PRODUCTION EDITOR
Kim Gabriel

PROOFREADER
Daphne Durkee

PRODUCTION
Dave Korman
Dave Damstra

COVER DESIGN AND
CREATIVE CONCEPTS
Felix Nelson

SITE DESIGN
Stacy Behan

The Peachpit Team

ASSOCIATE PUBLISHER
Stephanie Wall

EXECUTIVE EDITOR
Steve Weiss

PRODUCTION MANAGER
Gina Kanouse

SENIOR PROJECT EDITOR
Sarah Kearns

PROOFREADER
Sheri Cain

COMPOSITOR
Amy Hassos

PUBLISHED BY
Peachpit Press

Copyright © 2003 by NAPP Publishing, Inc.
FIRST EDITION: December 2003

International Standard Book Number: 0-7357-1389-8

Library of Congress Catalog Card Number: 2003112146

08 07 06 05 04 03   7 6 5 4 3 2 1

Interpretation of the printing code: The rightmost double-digit number is the year of the book's printing; the rightmost single-digit number is the number of the book's printing. For example, the printing code 03-1 shows that the first printing of the book occurred in 2003.

Composed in Myriad, Minion, and Helvetica by NAPP Publishing

Printed in the United States of America

Trademarks

Warning and Disclaimer

www.peachpit.com
www.scottkelbybooks.com

For my "Mac Buddies":
Bill Carroll, Don Wiggins, Jim Patterson, Rod Harlan,
Jim Workman, Dick Theriault, Ken Pitt, Dave Moser, Lesa Snider, Terry White,
Dave Gales, Jim Nordquist, John Couch, Larry Becker, Jon Gales, Jim Goodman,
and all my friends at the Bay Area Macintosh Users Group (BAM).

Acknowledgments

Putting together a book like this takes a team of very talented, creative, and dedicated people. Not only did I have the good fortune of working with such a great group of Mac-loving fanatics, I now get the great pleasure of thanking them, and acknowledging their hard work and tireless dedication.

First, I'd like to thank my beautiful and amazing wife Kalebra, for putting a smile on my lips, and a song in my heart, each and every day. She's part wonderwoman, part supermom, part business exec, and part stand-up comic. She makes every day a wonderful new experience, and I'm the luckiest guy in the world to have her.

I also want to thank my son Jordan. He's my special "little buddy" who's graced with his mom's smile, her love of life, and her true loving heart. The two of them bring an immeasureable amount of joy into my life and I'm very grateful God has blessed me with them.

Special thanks go to my contributing author Dave Gales, whose invaluable contributions to the book helped make it better in so many ways. Thanks for all your research, organizational skills, creative ideas, and dedication to the project.

To Dave Moser, for convincing me a few years ago to go beyond writing pro-Mac articles, and start writing pro-Mac books.

To Felix Nelson, for his ideas, his input, his great cover art, and for lending his overall creative talents to this book.

To the action-packed Lesa Snider (a.k.a. "the Yellow Rose of Texas"), for agreeing to tech edit the book in the midst of a dozen other projects. Clearly, she is a "Love Otter."

To Dick Theriault, the royal Macintosh book editor, for his priceless contributions to the book, and for once again letting us pull him kicking and screaming out of retirement.

Thanks to my editor Steve Weiss at Peachpit Publishing. It takes a measureable amount of guts to publish a book that steps outside the boundaries of traditional Mac books, and my hat's off to him for having the vision to see where and how it fits in, and for his singular vision of "just wanting to make great books." Also, special thanks to Rachel Tiley at New Riders, an unsung hero of book publishing.

I couldn't do any of this without the help and support of my wonderful assistant Kathy Siler. She's got an amazing attitude, except during football season when the Redskins are losing, which is fairly often as of late, but that's clearly not my fault.

To my brother Jeff, for being such an important part of my life, for becoming a part of our team, and for being a brother all other brothers should be judged by. You da man!

To Dave Damstra and Dave Korman for making the layout squeaky clean, and to Kim Gabriel for organizing the whole thing, and giving all the words another good workout.

Thanks to the whole team at KW Media Group, for their committment to excellence, for refusing to accept limitations, and for being an example of what's best about this industry.

To my friends and business partners Jim Workman and Jean A. Kendra for their support and enthusiasm for all my writing projects.

And most importantly, an extra special thanks to God and His son Jesus Christ for always hearing my prayers, for always being there when I need Him, and for blessing me with a wonderful life I truly love, and such a warm, loving family to share it with.

About the Author

Scott Kelby

Scott is Editor-in-Chief and co-founder of Mac Design Magazine, *Editor-in-Chief of* Photoshop User *magazine, and president of the National Association of Photoshop Professionals, the trade association for Adobe® Photoshop® users. Scott is also president of KW Media Group, Inc., a Florida-based software training and publishing firm.*

Scott is author of the books Macintosh: The Naked Truth, Mac OS X Killer Tips, Photoshop CS Down & Dirty Tricks, The Photoshop CS Book for Digital Photographers, *and* Photoshop 7 Killer Tips, *all from New Riders Publishing. He's a contributing author to the books* Photoshop Effects Magic, *also from New Riders;* Maclopedia, the Ultimate Reference on Everything Macintosh *from Hayden Books; and* Adobe Web Design and Publishing Unleashed *from Sams.net Publishing.*

Scott is Training Director for the Adobe Photoshop Seminar Tour, Technical Conference Chair for the Mac Design Conference, and he is a speaker at graphics trade shows and events around the world. Scott is also featured in a series of Adobe Photoshop video training tapes and DVDs and has been training Mac users and graphics professionals since 1993.

For more background info, visit www.scottkelby.com.

Contributing Author

Dave Gales

Dave is Systems Coordinator for KW Media Group, a Florida-based software training and publishing firm. He helps produce the Adobe Photoshop Seminar Tour, as well as the PhotoshopWorld conference (the annual convention of the National Association of Photoshop Professionals).

Dave is also founder and president of LifeMap Media, a creative firm that develops rich media resources and creative graphics for churches and small businesses. As president, he is able to combine his 20 years of experience as a local church pastor, his passion for clearly communicating God's story, his background as a professional photographer, and his long-time love for gadgets—Macintosh computers, in particular—to create working solutions for the firm's clients.

Table of Contents

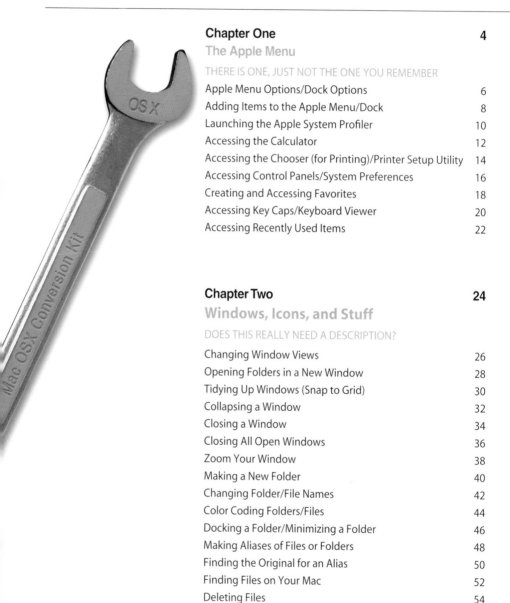

Table of Contents

Table of Contents

Chapter Ten   212

Don't Freak Out

INSTALLING MAC OS X, AND OTHER SCARY STUFF

Chapter Eleven   224

20 Cool Little Things You Couldn't Do in Mac OS 9

Chapter Twelve246

20 Little Things Apple Changed Just to Mess with Your Head

ACTUALLY, THERE'S A METHOD BEHIND THEIR MADNESS.
AT LEAST THAT'S WHAT WE'VE BEEN LED TO BELIEVE.

Start Here
(Or face the consequences)

Does the world really need another Mac OS X book?

I had to ask myself the exact same question. After days of careful research and hours of intense and personal soul searching, I came to the conclusion that yes, the world does need at least one more Mac OS X book. This book. However, after this book is written, it will then be okay for federal officials to close the Mac OS X book market, allowing no more Mac OS X books to be written (unless it is determined by an unbiased board, made up of myself and a hand-picked group of my closest friends and family members, that indeed another Mac OS X book is necessary).

Why this book?

Because it's different, and handles things from a different perspective that will help different people in a different way (are you picking up a theme here?). Here's what I mean: In my opinion, David Pogue's *Mac OS X: The Missing Manual* is the best book out there for learning Mac OS X. It's so complete, so thorough (at over 700 pages), and so well written, it really has no peer. So it would be pretty dumb for me to write that kind of book—the "best of breed" is already out there. But there is a book missing. A book for people who don't have the time to read David's book and take advantage of its depth. A book for people who need to start actually using Mac OS X today, and then sometime down the road (next week, next month, etc.), they'll get around to learning all the ins and outs; but for today, they just need to get up and around in Mac OS X.

Who are these people? People like my wife. She was part of the inspiration for this book, because after years of using various and sundry versions of Mac OS 7, 8, and 9, she finally upgraded to OS X (solely to take advantage of iPhoto, and the built-in ease of downloading photos from her Nikon digital camera).

Well, once it was installed, she went right to work, and within a few minutes she starting asking the usual questions—"Where's the Trash Can?" "Where are the Control Panels?" "How do I set the time?" and so on. I told her, "Honey, I've got a copy of David Pogue's book; you can read it tonight." She looked at me with total disdain, and said, "Do I really have to read a whole book? I didn't read a book to learn OS 9, can't you just show me?" This isn't the kind of thing an author likes to hear from his wife, so I tried to convince her it would be easy: "Sweetie, it's a great book, just spend a few hours with it." She gave me that "You don't get it" look, so I just answered a few more of her questions as they came up. More stuff along the lines of "Where'd they move the DVD player?" to "How do I change the system volume?" until finally she said something that changed everything. She said, "Ya know, you should write a book that just shows how to do the things you used to do in 9, but how to do them in X."

She's not nearly the Mac geek that I am, and even though I could put into her hands a copy of David's book that we already own, she just wouldn't read it, because she simply doesn't care. She needs to know the handful of things she wants to know, and outside of that, she just doesn't care. She doesn't care that's there a utility for setting your MIDI devices, or that there's a System Preference for remapping your keyboard to Croatian. She just wants to do what she

1

always did in 9, but now she wants to do it in X. It makes perfect sense. I think, as Mac authors, we generally write books that we would buy—books for Mac geeks that want to know all the tiniest little details, because we love this stuff. We crave it, we eat it up, we can't get enough. On the other hand, my wife (and countless others like her) can get enough. This book is for them. Well, not just for them; it's also for people who will buy a book like David's (timesaving tip: just buy David's) and read it at their leisure to uncover all the magic of X. But for now, they just need to get up and running right away. This is the definitive "get up and running right away" Mac OS X book for OS 8/9 users. It's actually the perfect complement to David's *Missing Manual* (but remember, if you can only buy one, buy mine—because at this point, David probably has more money than Belgium's gross national product).

So what makes this book different?

I knew you where going to ask that. Well, first off, this book has a very specific audience—people who are familiar with Mac OS 8 or 9. If you just bought your first Mac—this book isn't for you, because you need to have already used Mac OS 8 or 9 to get anything out of it. Secondly, this book doesn't tell you everything about Mac OS X. In fact, it tells you only a small amount—just what you need to know, to do in Mac OS X the same things you did back in Mac OS 9.

Is this book for you?

That depends. Do you have $29.99? (Kidding. Sort of.) Actually, it's for you if you need to start using Mac OS X today, and you can wait to learn all of the hidden, advanced, and cool other things it can do until some other time that's more convenient for you. Now, will I tell anyone if that time never comes? No. Your secret's safe with me. However, Mac OS X is pretty darn amazing, and by only reading this book, you'd be depriving yourself of learning from other great books, like the best-selling *Mac OS X Killer Tips*, from my favorite author (me), published by New Riders Publishing (ISBN: 0735713936).

Is this book for switchers?

Nope. This is NOT designed for people switching from PCs to Macs. This book is ONLY for people already using Macs and some version of Mac OS 8 or 9.

Oh come on, please?

No.

What if I am willing to pay more than the cover price?

Well, now. . . . No, no I can't do it. It's a specific book for specific people (speaking specifically).

Do you have to read the book in any order?

Absolutely not. I organized the book by topic, so you can use it more like a reference manual. For example, if you need to know how to adjust the brightness of your monitor, look in the Table of Contents, in the Monitors chapter. Remember, this book is there as your buddy, to help you find the things you're looking for in Mac OS X. So don't sit down and read it cover-to-cover. Instead, just keep it by your Mac, and at the first sign of "Hmmmm, where did they put that?" just grab the book and the answer is seconds away.

What if I'm installing Mac OS X myself?

Good luck! Actually, the installation process is very easy—it's having the answers to the questions that the Mac OS X Installer Assistant asks you along the way that is tricky. Although this book was designed to pick up after the installation (using Mac OS X, not installing it), I did include some things from the installation process that, if nothing more, might keep you from reaching a level of frustration that sends you climbing into a tower with a high-powered rifle and picking off pedestrians. Just look near the back of the book for the chapter titled "Don't Freak Out."

How to use this book

It's very important to me that you get the most from this book, and to do that you have to "get inside my head." (Don't worry, there's plenty of room in there, because I have a spacious über head, which can comfortably accommodate a typical family of four.)

I put this book together from a Mac OS 9 user's point of view, so for example there's a chapter called "Monitors" because that's what Mac OS 9 users refer to their monitor as—a monitor (even though Apple now calls your monitor a "display" in Mac OS X).

So, to use this book, just turn to the page that has the thing that you want to do in 9. On the left page, it shows (simply as a reminder) how you used to do that task in Mac OS 9, and the right page shows you how you do that same task now in Mac OS X. If Mac OS X offers some new features for that particular task (and in many cases, it does), I included those at the bottom in a little call-out box named "new stuff" (quite a striking name, dontchathink?).

Also, although this book will work almost equally well for Mac OS 8.5, 8.6, 9.0, 9.1, and 9.2 users (because those OS versions are all so similar), for the sake of sheer brevity, I always refer to the "old version" as Mac OS 9.

One more organizational thing: Some techniques appear twice (giving you a déjà vu effect). That's because I figured you might go looking in different places for different things. I'd rather have you see something twice than have you miss seeing it.

Another thing you might notice is that I often refer to the most recent version of Mac OS X as "Panther" (its Apple-given code name) rather than always referring to it by its full official name "Mac OS X version 10.3." I do that for two reasons: (1) In real life, I never refer to it as "Mac OS X version 10.3" and (2) this is real life. Besides, Panther sounds cooler than Mac OS X v10.3 (just ask Apple's marketing department).

What about the scary UNIX stuff?

This book contains no scary UNIX stuff. Since there was no UNIX in Mac OS 8/9, I can't show you how to do it in Mac OS X. Remember, this book is "how to do what you did in Mac OS 8/9, in Mac OS X." If it wasn't in Mac OS 9, it's not in this book. Except….

Except what?

Well, except I wanted to whet your appetite for some of the cool things Mac OS X can do, so I included a chapter called "20 Cool Little Things You Couldn't Do in Mac OS 9." I also included a chapter called "20 Little Things Apple Changed Just to Mess with Your Head." I also included some Quick Reference pages, with shortcuts to get you right where you want to go, after you've had a chance to work with the book a little bit. See, I care.

Is it time?

It's time. Have at it. Dive right in. Etc.

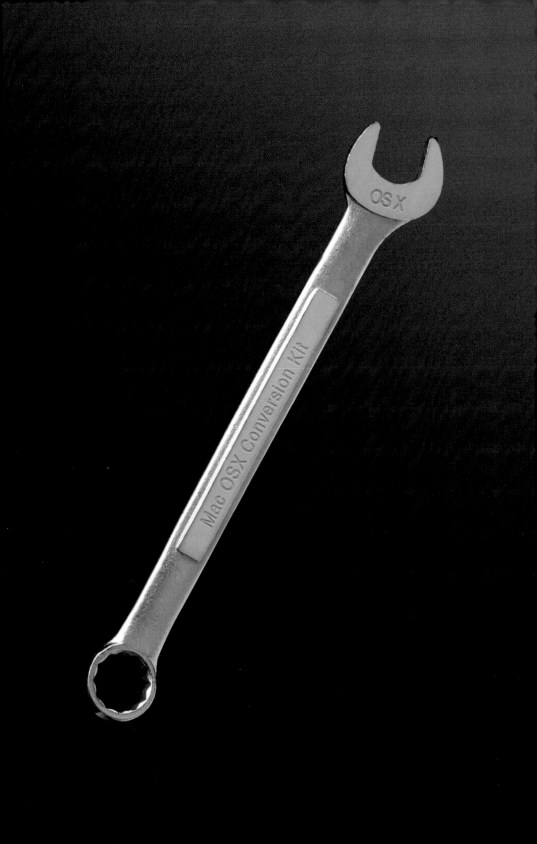

Chapter One

Legend has it that deep beneath Apple's Cupertino headquarters is a hidden cave where members of a secret cult of Apple system engineers don their sacred gowns for their trip deep into the darkest hidden passageway to reach "the

The Apple Menu

THERE IS ONE, JUST NOT THE ONE YOU REMEMBER

weirding room." Stories are told of meetings where they gather in a circle, and one engineer whispers the name of a deeply loved and respected aspect of the Apple operating system, and they all begin to laugh that we're-deep-in-a-secret-cave laugh that only people deep in a secret cave can laugh. Then they begin their ritual "changing-the-command" chant, where they each try to conjure up the most hideous, most insidious, yet deceivingly clever change they could implement that would cause nothing short of certain madness for longtime Macintosh users. The most famous of these sacred gatherings is the one where supposedly the engineer in the center of the ring whispered, "New folder shortcut," then after the appropriate amount of sinister cackling and macabre laughter, one engineer stood in the light of the flickering torches and said, "Let's make them add the Shift key (they all gasped), but better yet, let's use the *old* keyboard shortcut to open a new Finder window. Surely, my brothers, this will have the desired effect." They stood, cheered, and waved their chunks of freshly killed swine in the air. This engineer then became their king. And that's why today, even some of the most time-honored shortcuts and features have been changed, and that's exactly why this chapter exists: to show you where they've moved to now (by secret decree).

Apple Menu Options OS 9

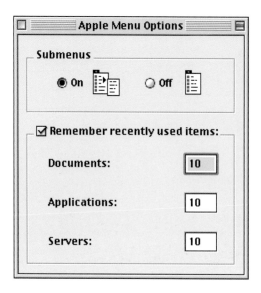

OS 9: Back in OS 9, you didn't have a lot of options for how your Apple menu worked. Basically, if you went under the Apple menu into the Control Panels folder and chose Apple Menu Options, you got the Control Panel shown above. This let you turn on/ off submenus, and let you determine how many recently used documents, applications, and servers would be displayed within the appropriate folders in the Apple menu. Pretty exciting stuff.

[Are Now] Dock Options OS X

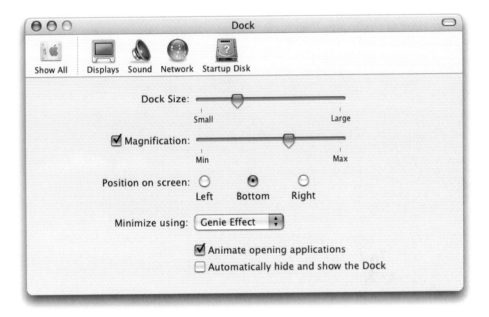

OS X: Now that the Dock has replaced the old Apple menu, you have a host of options, including control over the Dock's size, whether the icons magnify when you roll your mouse over them, and even the Dock's position on your screen. You can choose which effect will be used when you minimize a window to the Dock, and can toggle on/off the annoying little bouncing that occurs when you launch an application. You have the option of keeping the Dock visible at all times, or having it hidden, only appearing when your cursor moves over the area where the Dock would normally be. As for the stuff that used to be in the Apple Menu options for Mac OS 9, there are no sub-menu controls—if you want to see a list of what's in a folder in the Dock, just Control-click on it.

Adding Items to the Apple Menu OS 9

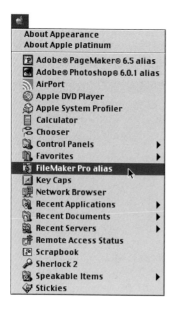

OS 9: Back in OS 9, to add an application to the Apple menu (for convenient launching), you'd start by locating the application file, then click on it and press Command-M to make an alias. Then, you'd open the System Folder, find the Apple Menu Items folder, drop the alias in there, and that alias would be added to the Apple menu. Sounds kind of like a pain, and it was.

Adding Items to [Now Called] the Dock OS X

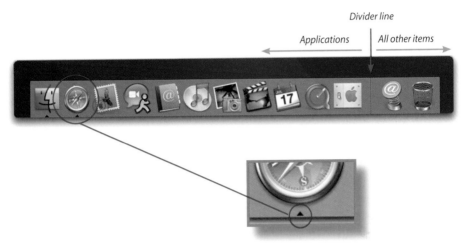

Divider line

Applications | All other items

A triangle under an icon indicates that the
application is open.

OS X: In Mac OS X, not only can you put just about anything in the Dock for quick access—it is incredibly easy to do. To put an application in the Dock, locate it on your drive and drag its icon to the Dock. Mac OS X automatically makes an alias that stays in the Dock. You can do the same with folders, individual documents, songs—anything you want. Do you connect to a server every day? Drag it to the Dock. Web site? No problem. Click on the URL in your Web browser and drag it to the Dock. It's a beautiful thing. There is one rule: Only applications can be placed to the left of the Dock's divider line. Any other type of file must go to the right. If you try to put something where it doesn't belong (and I know you will because you're a Mac user), it won't work.

new stuff:	*Now, when you launch an application, its icon temporarily appears in the Dock. If you want to keep an alias of this application in the Dock (for easy one-click launching), just Control-click on the application's Dock icon and choose Keep In Dock from the pop-up menu.* 

Launching the Apple System Profiler OS 9

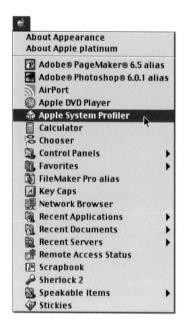

OS 9: To launch the Apple System Profiler back in Mac OS 9, you'd go under the Apple menu and choose Apple System Profiler. This would launch the utility and present a complete profile of your system software and hardware (particularly helpful to Apple service techs, who'll ask for info from this utility if you ever have a problem that requires service).

Launching the Apple System Profiler OS X

OS X: Now, you can access the Apple System Profiler by going under the Apple menu and choosing About This Mac. When the About window appears, click on the button for More Info to launch the Apple System Profiler. (It doesn't say that pressing that button will launch the Apple System Profiler, but it does. Freaky, I know.)

new stuff:	*Above, I showed the easiest way to access the Apple System Profiler, but if you were in the mood to dig around instead, it's actually found within the Utilities folder, which is within the Applications folder.*

Accessing the Calculator OS 9

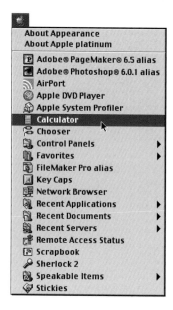

OS 9: Apple's age-old calculator (I call it "age-old" because it has looked exactly the same for as long as I've used a Mac) is found under the Apple menu in OS 9. Just choose Calculator, and up comes that tiny awful-looking gray and black calculator shown above. However, if you went to your Utilities folder and opened the Graphing Calculator, you were in for a treat. I would put that baby in demo mode and watch it create beautiful shapes for hours. The main problem with the Graphing Calculator was that you had to have an I.Q. high enough to boil water in order to use it, which probably explains why it was left out of Mac OS X.

Accessing the Calculator OS X

OS X: The calculator has undergone an extreme makeover in Mac OS X, but there's a lot more to it than just a pretty face. Menu options allow you to convert just about anything to anything else, have your Mac speak the numbers you're keying in, view a "paper tape," set precision up to 16 digits, and perform calculations in other popular formats (Hexadecimal, Binary, Octal , ASCII, Unicode, and last, but certainly not least, the ever-popular IEEE Hexadecimal).

new stuff:	*If you've got a big über-brain for math, go under the View menu and choose Advanced to reveal the added functionality of the OS X calculator. Note: If you find yourself using Advanced mode often, it might explain why you didn't have a date for the prom.*

Accessing the Chooser (for Printing) OS 9

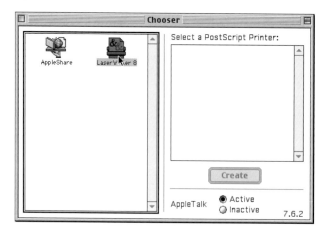

OS 9: Back in OS 9, before you could print a document, you'd have to go to the Chooser and tell your Mac which printer you wanted to use. If you had only one printer, you only had to do this once, and then your Mac would remember it next time. But if you had multiple printers, you'd wind up in the Chooser fairly often. To use the Chooser, you went to the Apple menu and selected Chooser. In the Chooser window, a list of print drivers appeared in the left column. When you clicked on one, a list of connected printers that used that driver appeared in the right window. You selected the one you wanted to use and closed the Chooser. If you ever wanted to print to a different printer, you had to go through this process again. Like I said, if you had multiple printers, you got pretty good at using the Chooser.

[Now Called] Printer Setup Utility OS X

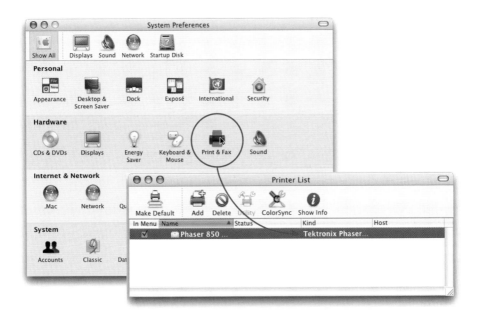

OS X: There is no Chooser in Mac OS X. To select printer options, you now use the Printer Setup Utility (a name which, frankly, makes much more sense to new users). From the Apple menu, select System Preferences and choose Print & Fax. When the pane opens, click on the Set Up Printers button and the Printer Setup Utility launches. A list of printers connected to your Mac (or available on your network) appears and you can choose the one you want to use by simply clicking on its name. If no printers appear, click the Add button and you can search for any printers that are available to add to your list of active printers.

new stuff: *Back in the day (two years ago), it seemed like everyone had a fax machine. But like a good $4 latté, they're getting harder to find these days. No problem if you use Panther. If you can print it, you can fax it. You probably had a sneaking suspicion already since it's named the Print & Fax preference pane, but I don't mind restating the obvious—obviously.*

Accessing Control Panels OS 9

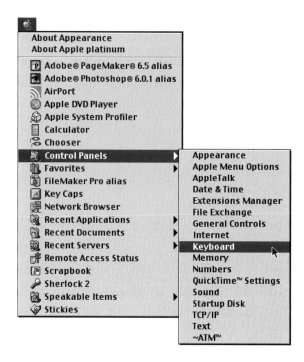

OS 9: Back in Mac OS 9, the fastest way to get to the System's Control Panels was to go under the Apple menu to Control Panels. If you paused for a second, a submenu opened (as shown above) and you could choose a Control Panel to open.

[Now Called] System Preferences OS X

OS X: In Mac OS X, Control Panels have been replaced by System Preferences (shown above). To access them, go to the Apple menu and choose System Preferences. Click on any individual item in System Preferences to reveal its preference pane. By default, the preferences are arranged by category. If you would rather see them arranged alphabetically, from the menu bar, select View and choose Organize Alphabetically from the drop-down menu.

Creating and Accessing Favorites OS 9

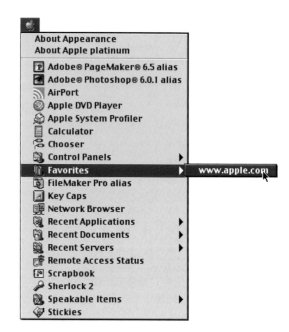

OS 9: In Mac OS 9, when you wanted to add a document or folder to your Favorites, you clicked once on its icon, went to the menu bar, and selected File. From the drop-down menu, you then selected Add to Favorites. Of course, if you didn't need to impress the person looking over your shoulder by making something simple look like rocket science, you could always just click on the document's icon and press Command-T. Not very impressive, but fast. To access your Favorites, you'd just go under the Apple menu, look in the Favorites folder, and it would be there.

Creating and Accessing Favorites OS X

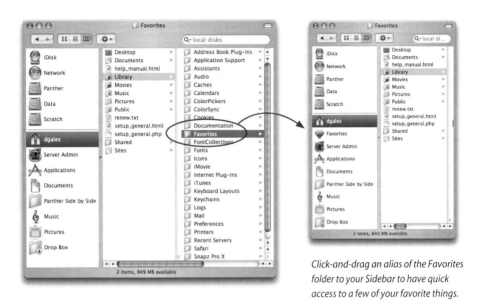

Click-and-drag an alias of the Favorites folder to your Sidebar to have quick access to a few of your favorite things.

OS X: There's a Favorites folder in Mac OS X, but it's not readily accessible. (Please, no cracks about why Apple would include a Favorites folder and then bury it deeper than a certain ruthless dictator recently buried certain weapons he said he didn't have.) If you want to use the official super-secret stealth Favorites folder, click on your User folder in the Sidebar, then click on Library. When your User Library opens, you'll see the Favorites folder sitting there right above FontCollections. Click-and-drag it to your Sidebar (actually, you're dragging an alias of the folder to your Sidebar—the real one stays undercover in your Library). Once you drop the Favorites folder in the Sidebar, notice that the folder icon changes to a red heart. To add an item to your Favorites as an alias in Mac OS X, just locate its icon, hold the Option and Command keys, and click-and-drag it onto the Favorites icon on your Sidebar.

Accessing Key Caps OS 9

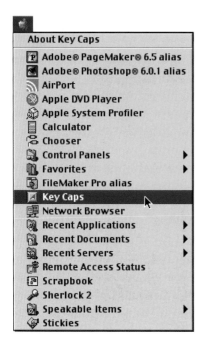

OS 9: Back in OS 9, to access Key Caps (the utility that let you find the keyboard loca-
tions for hidden font characters, like ©, ™, and é), you'd go under the Apple menu and
choose Key Caps. That brought up the Key Caps utility (shown above right), which
looks like a tiny keyboard. Once open, you could hold the Option or Shift key (or
both) and the mini-keyboard would then display the characters that would appear
if you typed a letter with that modifier key held down. For example, if you held the
Option key down and looked at the Key Caps keyboard, you'd see that the letter G
now displayed the © symbol. So then you'd know that pressing Option-G on your real
keyboard would give the copyright symbol (©).

[Now Called] Keyboard Viewer OS X

Keyboard Viewer

Keyboard Viewer with Option key

OS X: Key Caps is replaced by Keyboard Viewer in Mac OS X. Before you can access it, you have to activate it by going to the Apple menu, choosing System Preferences, and selecting International. When the Preference pane opens, click the Input Menu button and check the box next to Keyboard Viewer and the Show Input Menu in the Menu Bar box located in the lower-left corner of the pane. Now, whenever you want to find the key combination for a special character, click on the Input menu icon on the right side of your menu bar and select Show Keyboard Viewer from the drop-down menu. Select the font you are using by clicking on the pop-up menu at the bottom of the Keyboard Viewer, then press the various modifier keys (Shift, Control, Option, and Command), and you will see the characters that are available. *Warning*: Unlike Key Caps in Mac OS 9, the keys in Keyboard Viewer are "live." What that means is that if you're working on a document and open Keyboard Viewer to find a keyboard combination, any key or key combination you press will actually be input into your application if you have an active cursor or selected text.

Accessing Recently Used Items OS 9

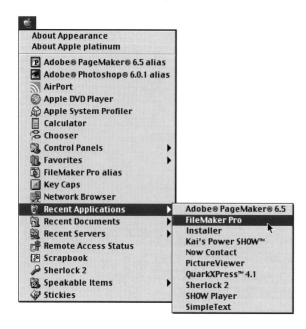

OS 9: Back in Mac OS 9, two folders in the Apple menu gave you convenient access to the files and applications you most recently used. To access these, you'd just go under the Apple menu to the folder named Recent Applications or Recent Documents (as shown above) and choose the recently used application or file you want to open.

Accessing Recently Used Items OS X

OS X: Now there's just one menu item for accessing both recently used applications and documents. Go under the Apple menu and choose Recent Items. An alphabetical menu opens, listing recent applications first, followed by recent documents. Just scroll to the item you want to open.

new stuff:	In Mac OS X, Apple has added a new command that you can find at the bottom of the Recent Items list. It's called Clear Menu and it does exactly what it says—clears the list of both recently used applications and documents. So when you're finished playing Quake, select Clear Menu, then launch and quit Photoshop, Maya, and Final Cut Pro. The next person to use your Mac will be very impressed.

Chapter Two

One of the things that Apple didn't change "a whole bunch" (that's a technical term) is how windows, icons, and stuff (another technical term) work in Mac OS X. Oh, don't you worry, they moved just enough stuff around to make you

Windows, Icons, and Stuff

DOES THIS REALLY NEED A DESCRIPTION?

feel ill-at-ease for a few days, but not enough that you'll think you're using Windows XP. This chapter (dedicated to authors everywhere who, when faced with the problem of coming up with a word to describe certain elements of a computer operating system, rather than going through the time-consuming research route, opted instead to use the word "stuff") looks at how these things have changed, from the subtle nuances to the…the…ah heck, they're all subtle nuances, but they're not so subtle that you wouldn't notice; yet they're subtle enough to subtly remind you that things have changed. I'm rambling again, aren't I? Look, here's what it comes down to—I couldn't come up with anything particularly clever to say about windows, icons, and stuff, and frankly, if I hadn't used the word "stuff" in the title and found a way to work the word "subtle" into this chapter intro several times, this would be just a couple of lines of copy, and then my editor would have insisted that I write more. Now I can get away with this rambling because I know for a fact that editors don't read chapter intros—they just look to see that a reasonable amount of text is there. Perhaps even random words. Let's see: Fishbarn cement cow seaweed dander. See, they never check this stuff. *[Oh, yes they do! And it isn't easy. –Ed.]*

Changing Window Views OS 9

OS 9: Back in Mac OS 9, you had your choice of three views: Icon view, List view, and the always popular (among the eight people who actually used it) Big Ugly Button view. The default was Icon view, but if you wanted to switch to one of the others, you would just choose As List or As Buttons from the View menu on the Finder's menu bar.

0

Changing Window Views OS X

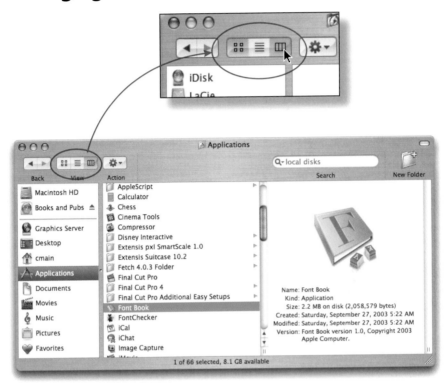

OS X: In Mac OS X, you still have three choices: Icon view, List view, and the new and wonderful Column view. At the top of every Finder window, you see the three View buttons (circled above). The first (from the left) is for viewing your window contents by icon. The second (middle button) is for List view, and click the third for the new Column view. *Note:* If the View buttons aren't visible, just click the clear pill-shaped button at the top far right of the window's title bar.

new stuff:	The Column view is new to Macintosh, and many people like it so much it's the only view they use, because they claim they can get to where they want faster by moving left to right, rather than digging through folders.

Opening Folders in a New Window OS 9

OS 9: In Mac OS 9, you really didn't have a choice about this; any time you opened a folder, it opened its own separate window. This made for a lot of open windows (which tended to clutter your desktop), but it made copying files from one window to another pretty effortless.

Opening Folders in a New Window OS X

OS X: Now, in Mac OS X, by default when you open a folder, it doesn't open a new window. Instead, the contents of the folder replace the contents of the current window. To change the default, make sure you're in the Finder by clicking anywhere on the desktop, then from the menu bar at the top of your screen, click on Finder and select Preferences from the drop-down menu. Click on the General icon at the top of the dialog, check the "Always open folders in a new window" box, and then close the Preference pane. If you ever want to override the default without changing the Finder Preferences, just hold down the Command key and double-click on the folder that you want to open in a new window.

new stuff:	*If you hold the Option key when clicking on a folder, it not only opens the folder in its own separate window, but it also immediately closes the original window where the folder resided.*

Tidying Up Windows (Snap to Grid) OS 9

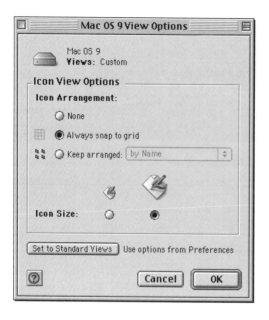

OS 9: In Mac OS 9, to have the icons in your open window snap to an invisible grid (handy for housekeeping purposes), you'd go under the View menu located on the Finder's menu bar and choose View Options (the shortcut was Command-J). The dialog pictured above presented you with several options that you could set to your liking for arranging the items on your desktop. The next time your desktop was a mess, all you had to do was click on the View menu and choose Clean Up and your desktop was instantly neat and organized.

Tidying Up Windows (Snap to Grid) OS X

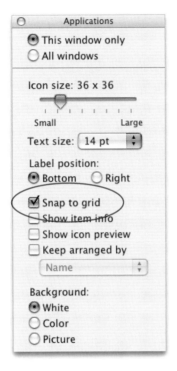

OS X: Now, to have the icons in your window (if you're in Icon view) snap to an invisible grid, press Command-J to bring up the View Options dialog (above), then turn on the checkbox for Snap to Grid. The name of the command might lead you to believe that your icons will instantly snap to the grid—they don't. If you're getting paid by the hour, grab each icon individually and drag them a bit. When you let go, they snap into place. Otherwise, select View from the menu bar and choose Clean Up from the pull-down menu. Now all your icons will line up to the grid at once.

new stuff: *When you turn on Snap to Grid, you'll see a tiny icon of a grid in the bottom left-hand corner of your window. You can turn on this option for just the currently open, active window or for all windows by clicking on the appropriate button at the top of the View Options dialog.*

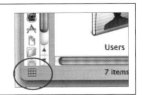

Collapsing a Window OS 9

To "unroll" a window, you simply double-clicked on the title bar of the collapsed window.

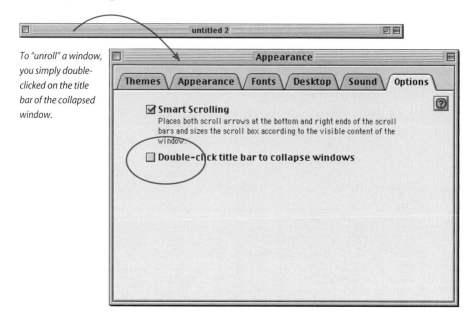

OS 9: In Mac OS 9, you could double-click on a window's title bar, and it would "roll up" like a window shade, leaving only the window's title bar still visible. To turn this function on, you'd go under the Apple menu, into the Control Panels folder, and choose Appearance. In the Appearance folder, you'd click on the Options tab and turn on the checkbox labeled Double-Click Title Bar to Collapse Windows.

Collapsing a Window OS X

OS X: Windowshading is no longer available in Mac OS X, but it's been replaced by something better—minimizing to the Dock. In the top-left corner of every window, there are three round buttons. (If you've kept the default Blue option in the Appearance preference pane, they're red, yellow, and green. If you've chosen the Graphite option, they're all gray.) When you want to clear a window from the desktop but want to be able to retrieve it quickly, click the yellow (or middle) button and the window shrinks down to the Dock (technically, this is called "minimizing"). When you want it back, click on its Dock image.

new stuff:	Start playing a Quick Time movie. While it's playing, click the yellow button to minimize it. Look at its image in the Dock. Yep, still playing! When you minimize a document's window, it remains active. Besides being cool, it's useful. If you are rendering an iMovie project, for instance, a quick glance at the Dock lets you know if it's done or still rendering.

Closing a Window OS 9

OS 9: To close a window in Mac OS 9, you'd click on the close box in its upper left-hand corner. You could also press Command-W as a shortcut (if you're too lazy to click, like me).

Closing a Window OS X

OS X: I know this one may seem a little "duh," but I've had people who've just switched to Mac OS X ask this one. They weren't the sharpest people mind you, but they did ask. Now, to close a window, you click on the red close button at the top far left, or you can still use the old Command-W shortcut to close the window via keyboard. Again, if you're charging by the hour, you could go under the Finder menu and choose Close Window, but as far as I can tell, that has actually only been used once in the history of Mac OS X, and then only by someone whose keyboard and mouse were both irreparably damaged, and he could only navigate by using the arrow keys on the keyboard; and even at that, he might have been lying. *Note:* Clicking the red close button closes the window, but does not quit the associated application. The application's icon remains in the Dock, and you will notice the triangle below it indicating that it's still running. There are some exceptions to this rule, however, which include System Preferences, the Calculator, and the Help Viewer.

Closing All Open Windows OS 9

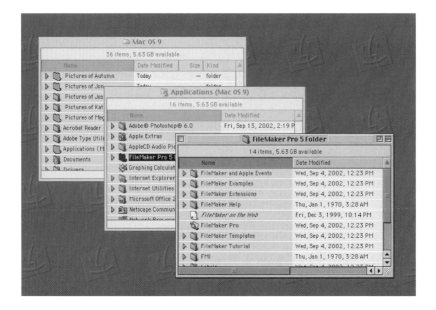

OS 9: In Mac OS 9, to quickly close every open window for a single application, you could Option-click on the close box in the upper-left corner of any open window, and all open windows for the same application would close.

Closing All Open Windows OS X

OS X: Now, you do pretty much the same thing—you Option-click on the red close button in the upper left-hand corner of the title bar and all open windows for that application close. You haven't quit the application, just closed all its windows.

Here are a couple more shortcuts that are handy when working with multiple windows: If you're working with several applications and want to see only the windows for one of them, Option-Command-click on the application's Dock icon. Any open windows for other applications become hidden. The beauty is, they're not closed. Click on their applications' Dock icons and they will be visible again. Option-clicking on the Dock icon of the active application will hide its windows. Click on it again and they're back.

new stuff:	*Want to minimize all the open windows for a particular application to the Dock? Option-click on the yellow (middle) button of one of them and they will all get sucked down to the Dock until you need them again.*

Zoom Your Window OS 9

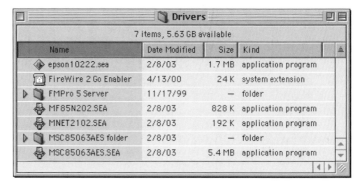

OS 9: Why is it that the picture you need to see or the information you need to copy off the screen is always covered up by a window that takes up half your screen? In Mac OS 9, if you wanted to instantly make a window smaller (or larger), all you had to do was go to the upper right-hand corner of its title bar, locate the two little square boxes, and click on the one on the left. I always called it "That little box in the top right-hand corner of the window," but for the geeks among you who like to use the technical terms for things, it's officially known as the Zoom Box. If your window is big, it zooms it small. If it's small, it zooms it big.

Zoom Your Window OS X

OS X: Now, to zoom an open window in Mac OS X, you click on the green zoom button (the third button from the left) at the upper left-hand corner of your window's title bar. This button seems kind of lame, but it may save you someday. In Mac OS X, you can only resize windows by clicking-and-dragging them at the bottom right-hand corner. Every now and then, you get a window that somehow gets bigger than your screen (I suspect it's steroids, but I've never been able to prove it) and you can't grab the bottom right-hand corner to resize it. When this happens, just click the green button and your window shrinks until it fits on your screen again, allowing you to resize it.

new stuff:	*Just in case you forget which little window button does what: If you put your cursor over any one of the buttons, they'll give you a hint. As you roll over them, an "X" appears over the red button (letting you know that this closes the window); a minus sign appears over the yellow button (letting you know that clicking it will minimize the window); and a plus (+) sign appears over the green button, letting you know that clicking on it will maximize (zoom) the window.*

Making a New Folder OS 9

OS 9: In Mac OS 9, there were two ways to make a new folder. The first was to go to the File menu and select New Folder. Now, actually choosing this from the menu (rather than using the keyboard shortcut) is only for the wimpiest, scaredy-cat, big-baby, wuss-head, Mac user (not you of course, but surely you can think of a friend that fits that description). The power user (you, for example) would press Command-N to create a new folder. Simple. Easy. Elegant. It was actually the perfect keyboard shortcut. That's probably why Apple decided to change it in Mac OS X.

Making a New Folder OS X

OS X: Now, you press Shift-Command-N (I know, I know, how could they change this particular keyboard shortcut after all these years?), or you can simply Control-click on any open space within a Finder window (or on the desktop), and a pop-up menu appears allowing you to choose New Folder (as shown above). I prefer this method, partially as my own personal protest against using Shift-Command-N.

Changing Folder/File Names OS 9

OS 9: To change a folder name in Mac OS 9, the easiest way was either to click on the file *name* you wanted to change, or to click on the *icon* of the file and then press the Return key. Either action would highlight the name of the file for you, so all you had to do was type in a new name.

Changing Folder/File Names OS X

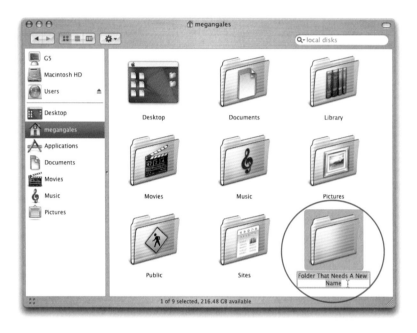

OS X: Now, when in Icon view or on the desktop, you can click directly on a file's name and it highlights, ready for you to type in a new name. In List or Column view, you click on an icon, then press the Return key to highlight it; but honestly, since you can click directly on the name in Icon view and it highlights, why would you want to click, then press Return? It's just extra work. Backbreaking work (if you will) and totally unnecessary.

new stuff:	If you're in no particular hurry, there's another way to change a file's name. Click on the file's icon, then press Command-I to bring up the file's Info window. Then, in the Info window, choose Name & Extension. This brings up a field where you can rename the file.	

Color Coding Folders/Files OS 9

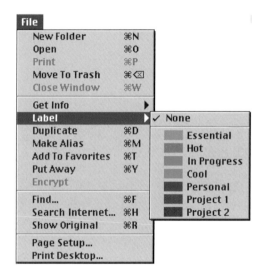

OS 9: Back in Mac OS 9, you could color code files by clicking on the icon of a file or folder, then you'd go under the File menu, under Label, and assign a color (as shown above).

Color Coding Folders/Files OS X

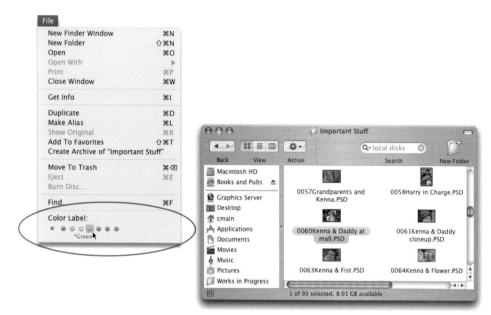

OS X: In Mac OS X, it's called Color Label, but it works much the same way. Click once on the document or folder you want to label to highlight it. Now, click File on the menu bar, select Color Label, and move your cursor over the color you want. In Mac OS 9, the icon itself changed color according to the color you chose. In Mac OS X, the name of the folder or file takes on the highlight color instead (see above).

new stuff: You can change the names of the labels by selecting Finder from the menu bar and choosing Preferences. Click on the Labels icon at the top and set things up just the way you want.

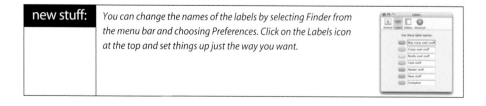

Docking a Folder to Bottom of Your Screen OS 9

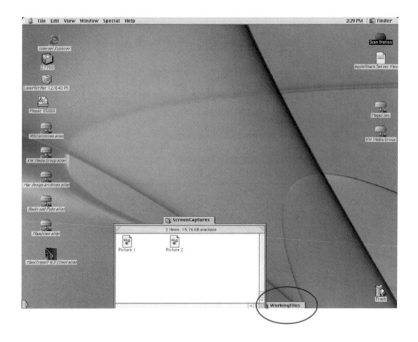

OS 9: Back in OS 9, once a window was open in the Finder, you could click on the title bar and drag it to the bottom of the screen, and it would stay there, with just a small tab sticking up. When you wanted to pop open that window again, you'd just click on the tab and it would appear on screen.

Minimizing a Folder to the Dock OS X

OS X: Now, you can add a folder or file to the bottom of your screen by minimizing it to the Dock. You do this by either clicking once on the yellow (center) button on the top left of any window, or by just pressing Command-M while the window is active. Then, to access the window again (have it pop up on screen), just click on it once in the Dock (as shown above). To let you know that a Dock icon is actually a minimized window, a tiny icon of the application that created the window is added to the lower right-hand corner of its Dock icon.

| new stuff: | If you want to turn off the Genie Effect that you see when you put items in the Dock, Control-click on the Dock's divider line. When the pop-up menu appears, select Minimize Using Scale Effect. | |

Making Aliases of Files or Folders OS 9

OS 9: Back in Mac OS 9, you'd click on the file that you wanted to make an alias of, then you'd press Command-M. You could also hold Option-Command while you dragged the folder or file for which you wanted to make an alias.

Making Aliases of Files or Folders OS X

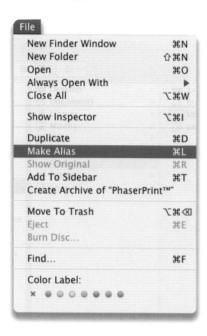

OS X: Now, you click on the file for which you want an alias, then press Command-L (the shortcut changed because the old Command-M shortcut is now used to minimize a window to the Dock). So why did I show the menu command above? Just to tease you. If you're not getting paid by the hour, here's a quicker way to make an alias. Hold down the Option and Command keys while you drag the file you want to make an alias of right out of the window it appears in. Instant alias. Drag it to either the desktop or another window or folder. It may not really be faster, but it's great for making lesser Mac users feel, well…lesser.

Finding the Original for an Alias OS 9

OS 9: Aliases are great—so great that you can accumulate hundreds of them on your hard drive and forget where the original files are saved. Back in Mac OS 9, when you needed to find the original file for an alias, you Control-clicked on the alias and chose Show Original from the contextual menu that opened. You could also click once on the alias to highlight it, then go to the File menu and choose Show Original (shown above).

Finding the Original for an Alias OS X

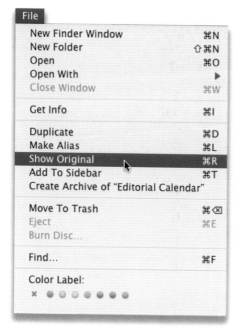

OS X: This function works the same as it did in Mac OS 9. Control-click on an alias and choose Show Original from the pop-up menu. If you prefer, you can also click once on the alias to highlight it, then go to the File menu and choose Show Original (shown above).

new stuff:	*If you hate Control-clicking (hey, some people do), you have an alternative. In Panther, you can click the Action button (located within the Finder window toolbar—its icon looks like a little gear) and you'll get a pop-up menu with a lot of the same commands as if you had Control-clicked on a file. It's ideal for anyone who suffers from Controlclickaphobia.*

Finding Files on Your Mac OS 9

OS 9: In Mac OS 9, to find a particular file on your Mac, you'd press Command-F to bring up Sherlock 2 (shown above), enter the file's name (or other attribute) into Sherlock's Find field, then press the Magnifying Glass button to the right of the Find field to start your search.

Finding Files on Your Mac OS X

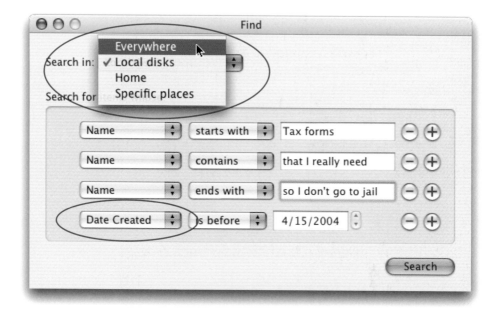

OS X: In Mac OS X, you still use Command-F, but it now opens the window shown above. (Sherlock is now only used for Internet searches.) You can refine your search by using the "Search in" and "Search for" pop-up menus available in the search window. An additional search feature in Mac OS X is a search entry field built right into the toolbar of every Finder window. Just start typing in the field and it starts searching immediately. If you want to change the parameters of the search, just click on the magnifying glass in the search field and you can choose to search Local Disks, Home, Selection, or Everywhere.

new stuff:	*Mac OS X (and many applications) install huge amounts of language support—some for languages I'm not sure are even spoken. Besides taking up space on your hard drive, they slow up things like searching because your Mac looks through all those files. Here's how to speed things up: From the Finder, go to the menu bar, select Finder, and choose Preferences. Click the Advanced icon and then on the Select button at the bottom of the dialog, you can select only the language(s) you want included in searches.*

Deleting Files OS 9

OS 9: To Delete a file in Mac OS 9, you'd drag it to the Trash icon at the bottom right-hand corner of your desktop (or wherever you kept it). The file was not actually deleted at this point—just sitting in the Trash. If you changed your mind, you could take it back out again. To delete the file, you had to choose Empty Trash from the Special menu (or Control-click on the Trash icon and select Empty Trash from the pop-up menu).

Deleting Files OS X

Since Mac OS X is designed to run in a multiuser environment, each user has his own Trash that other users can't access. If you fill your Trash then log out, it will still be waiting for you the next time you log in. It doesn't matter how many other people have logged in or whether they have emptied the Trash—your trash is still safe.

OS X: In Mac OS X, it's pretty much the same. You have to start by putting the file you want to delete in the Trash, but the Trash icon has moved. It's no longer at the bottom right-hand corner of your desktop. Instead, it's at the far right of the Dock (although a faster method of "trashing" a file is to just click on the file, then press Command-Delete, which places the file into the Trash for you lickety-split). Then, to actually delete the file and any others that are in the Trash, now you go under the Finder menu (rather than the Special menu, which no longer exists) and choose Empty Trash (or use the Empty Trash keyboard shortcut: Shift-Command-Delete).

| new stuff: | *Emptying the Trash only deletes the directory information that allows your Mac to find the files—all your data is still on your drive. New in Mac OS X is Secure Empty Trash, which overwrites the files you want to get rid of with random characters that even the CIA won't be able to crack. That being said, if you're concerned about the CIA reading your trash, you may have bigger problems than learning Mac OS X.* | |

Chapter Three

You may find it hard to believe, but people are different (this came as somewhat of a shock to me. I always assumed everybody was like me). However, once you think about it, it

Customizing Your Mac
SETTING UP YOUR SYSTEM TO YOUR TASTE

explains a lot of things (like *The Anna Nicole Show* and Monster Truck and Tractor pulls. Not everyone thinks those are as cool as I do, which I found disconcerting, to say the least). So it's entirely possible that once you start working with Mac OS X, you might be tempted to change some of the system preferences to suit your own tastes, needs, and work habits. Here's the thing: Don't do it. Why? Because only I am allowed to change the defaults. You see, as I mentioned earlier, people are different, and they basically fall into two categories: (1) you, and (2) me. Through a special arrangement with Apple's executive management, only I am allowed to change the user preferences of Mac OS X, because I am, after all, the different one. However, should you be feeling a bit "me-ish" and want a glimpse into what it's like being "me" (without all the limos, parties with P. Diddy, flowing Cristal, and paparazzi, of course), then turn the page to learn how to make your Mac, your way. You're so "me."

Setting the Date & Time OS 9

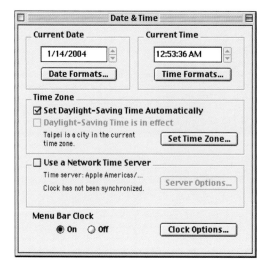

OS 9: Back in OS 9, to change the time or date, you'd go under the Apple menu, to the Control Panels folder, and choose Date & Time. You would set the time by highlighting the time fields and typing in the date and time (or by using the up/down arrow buttons).

Setting the Date & Time OS X

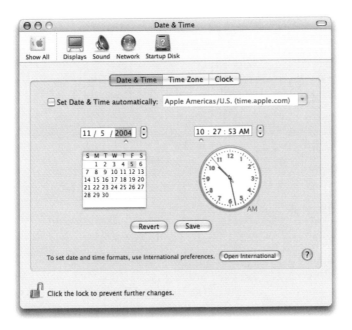

OS X: Now to set the Date & Time, you go under the Apple menu and choose System Preferences. When the System Preferences pane appears, click on the Date & Time icon, which brings up the pane shown above. Set the date or time by clicking on the item you want to change and typing in the new information (or clicking on the adjustment arrows.) Note that if you have selected Set Date & Time Automatically, the adjustment arrows won't appear. The date and time will be set automatically whenever you go online. *Geek Tip:* You can actually set the time by dragging the hands of the clock. Is this an efficient way to set the time? Hardly. But does it make you look cool? Oh yeah.

new stuff:	*You can also quickly get to the Date & Time preference pane by clicking-and-holding on the clock that appears in your menu bar (at the top-right corner of your screen). When the drop-down menu appears, choose Open Date & Time. It doesn't get much quicker than that.*

Setting the Number of Recent Apps OS 9

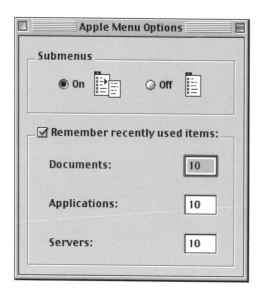

OS 9: Your Mac keeps track of the last applications and documents you opened. This is pretty handy, because many people wind up working in the same few applications, and often on the same document, over and over again. By remembering these recently used applications and documents, you can quickly jump right to the file you need, without having to dig around your hard drive, searching through folders, etc. Instead, if you want to open a recently used application, you go under the Apple menu, click-and-hold on the Recent Applications folder, and a list of your most recently used apps appears. It works the same way for documents. However, you get to decide just how many apps and documents your Mac keeps track of. Back in OS 9, you'd set the number of recently opened applications and documents by going under the Apple menu, to the Control Panels folder, and choosing Apple Menu Options. The somewhat cheesy-looking dialog above would appear, where you could type in the number of items you wanted your Mac to keep track of.

Setting the Number of Recent Apps OS X

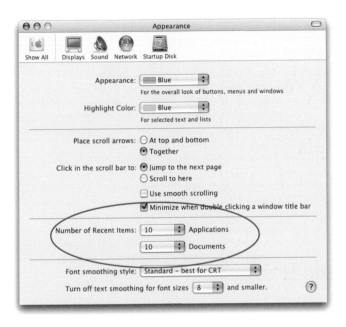

OS X: Now, you go under the Apple menu and choose System Preferences. Then, click on the Appearance icon to bring up the Appearance Preference pane, and in the section for Number of Recent Items, click on the pop-up menu (there's one for Applications and for Documents). Choose the number of recently used items you want your Mac to make available from the Apple menu's Recent Items menu. Now, when you go under the Apple menu and choose Recent Items, the list displays the number of recently used applications and documents you chose in the Preference pane.

new stuff: *When you use the Recent Items feature (not the preferences shown above, but the actual feature found under the Apple menu), at the very bottom of the list is something new—the menu command Clear Menu, which does just that—it clears all the recent applications or documents, and starts over.*

Changing the Highlight Color OS 9

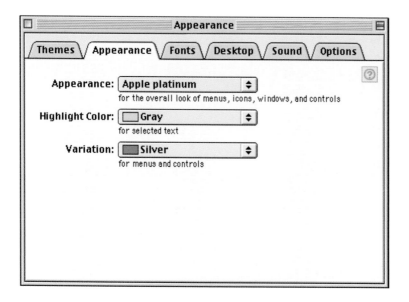

OS 9: When you click on an icon, the name of the file highlights in color (to let you know it's selected). You could change the color of this highlighting (and I always did) to any color you liked (I usually choose a vivid yellow, but hey, that's just me). Back in Mac OS 9, to change the Highlight Color, you'd go under the Apple menu, to the Control Panels folder, and choose Appearance. The dialog shown above would appear and you could select your desired color from the Highlight Color pop-up menu.

Changing the Highlight Color OS X

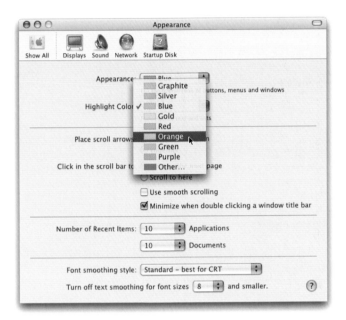

OS X: Now, you choose your Highlight Color from the Appearance Preference pane.
Go under the Apple menu and choose System Preference. When the Preference pane
appears, click on the Appearance icon to bring up its Preference pane. Near the top
is the Highlight Color pop-up menu. Choose your Highlight Color from the preset
colors shown here, or choose Other to pick your own custom Highlight color from a
pop-up Color Picker that appears.

Adjusting Overall Volume OS 9

OS 9: Back in Mac OS 9, to adjust the overall volume of your Mac, you'd go under the Apple menu, to the Control Panels folder, and choose Sound. When the Sound dialog appeared, you'd click on the Output tab to bring up the Output panel (as shown above). At the bottom of this panel is a slider that you'd use to adjust the volume or to mute the output volume entirely.

Adjusting Overall Volume OS X

OS X: Now, to adjust the overall volume of your Mac, click on the Apple menu, choose System Preferences, and select Sound. It doesn't matter which button you choose here, because the Output Volume slider appears at the bottom of all of them. (How's that for convenient?) Click on the adjustment slider on the Output Volume bar and move it left or right until the volume is at the level you want.

new stuff:	Want the ultimate in speed? The next time you have the Sound Preference pane open, click on the checkbox for Show Volume in Menu Bar. Now you can access the Output Volume slider right from the menu bar at the top right of your screen. You'll see a little black icon of a speaker—click once on it and a volume slider drops down (as shown at right). How cool is that?

Changing the System Font Size OS 9

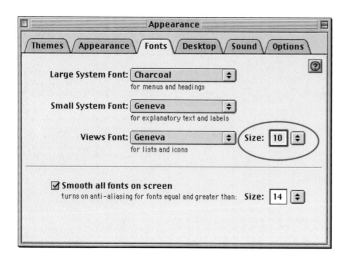

OS 9: If you're using a high-resolution monitor setting (and most new Macs' native screen resolution is so high that it makes your icons look miniature), chances are the text on screen is pretty darn small (like the text below icons, in lists, etc.). Back in Mac OS 9, you could change the size of your Views Font by going under the Apple menu in the Control Panels folder and choosing Appearance. In the Appearance dialog, you'd click on the Fonts tab, and there was a field for choosing your Views Font size (it's circled above).

Changing the System Font Size OS X

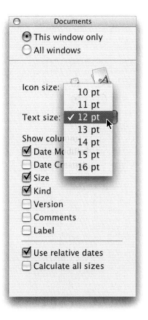

OS X: Now, when you're in Icon view or List view, you can choose the font size you'd like for any individual window (giving you the choice of having the text larger in some windows, smaller in others—the ultimate in font-size personalization). Just open the Finder window where you'd like to change the font size, then press Command-J (or click on View in the menu bar and choose Show View Options). When the View dialog opens, you see a pop-up menu with preset text sizes for you to choose from (as shown above). If you want to affect just this one window, choose This Window Only at the top of the View dialog. If you want to change sizes system-wide and haven't set any other windows to This Window Only, choose All Windows. In Column view, changing the text size affects all columns.

new stuff:	*Back in Mac OS 9, Apple let you easily change the system font and the size, but in OS X, you can only change the size. Why? Because they're evil, evil I tell you! (Which really means, I don't know, but it sounds much better than "I don't know.")*

Choosing Scroll Bar Arrows OS 9

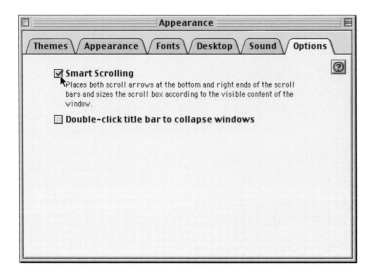

OS 9: By default, in any window that has scroll bars, the little scroll arrows (the ones you click to scroll up and down) are located at the top and bottom of the side scroll bar, and the far left and right of the bottom scroll bar. However, some people think it's more convenient to have both the up/down and left/right scroll arrows appear together, at the bottom-right corner of the active window. These people are freaks (just kidding). In Mac OS 9, this feature was called Smart Scrolling (only to make these freaks feel better about themselves. Again, just a joke. Sort of). To turn Smart Scrolling on, you went under the Apple menu, and in the Control Panels folder, chose Appearance. When the Appearance Preference panel appeared, you clicked on the Options tab (the far right one) and then on the checkbox for Smart Scrolling. This placed the scroll arrows together at the bottom-right corner of the window. It also automatically made the scroll box (that little box you drag around in the scroll bar) shrink and grow based on what proportion of the window was visible.

Choosing Scroll Bar Arrows OS X

OS X: Now, you turn this feature on/off by going under the Apple menu, choosing System Preferences, and clicking on the Appearance icon. The middle section has a Place Scroll Arrows option. Click the radio button for Together to place the scroll arrows together at the bottom-right corner of the window (or choose At Top and Bottom to do just that). In Mac OS X, the resizing of the scroller, or "thumb," is always on, regardless of which scroll arrow option you choose.

Changing Your Desktop Background OS 9

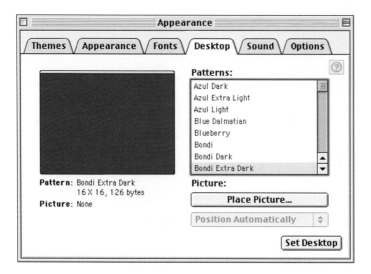

OS 9: To change the desktop background pattern in Mac OS 9, you'd go under the Apple menu, under Control Panels, and choose Appearance. When the Appearance panel appeared, you'd click on the Desktop tab and then you could choose one of the lame, I mean built-in, desktop patterns. There was also a button called Place Picture that let you choose a photo for your desktop background. Once you had the pattern or photo you wanted in the Preview window, to apply it as your desktop, you had to press the Set Desktop button at the bottom right of the dialog.

Changing Your Desktop Background OS X

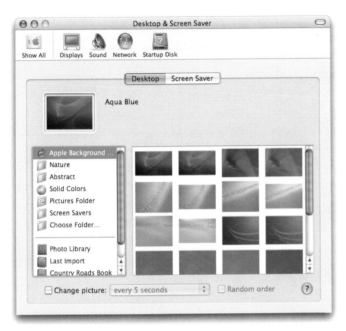

OS X: Now, you go under the Apple menu and choose System Preferences. When the Preference pane appears, click on the Desktop & Screen Saver icon to bring up its Preference pane (shown above). Click one of the available collections from the list at the left to see thumbnails of the images in that collection (you'll notice that you also have access to your iPhoto Library at the bottom of the list). To choose a desktop, just click on one of the thumbnails on the right. That's all there is to it. If you want to add one of your own images to the list, locate it on your drive and drag-and-drop it straight into the preview window at the top left of the pane. You don't have to move it to any special folder; Mac OS X remembers its location. Incidentally, there's no Set Desktop button like in the old days. Now, when you click on an image, it instantly becomes your desktop.

new stuff:	In Mac OS X, there's now a Change Picture option, and you can choose to have the system automatically choose a new desktop either at different time intervals, when your computer wakes from sleep, or when logging in. There's a Random Order checkbox (as shown above) to have your Mac choose a random desktop background each time; otherwise, it displays each new background in the order it appears in the scroll box.

Choosing Your Numbers Format OS 9

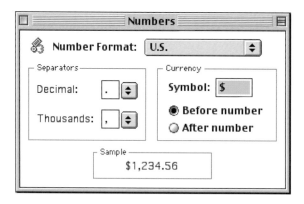

OS 9: You have the option of setting how your numbers are presented, based on which country you live in. For example, you'd choose which symbol is used to denote money, like $ or £, and whether the symbol goes before the number (like $1,500) or after it (like 1,500£). Back in OS 9, these were set by going under the Apple menu, inside the Control Panels folder, and choosing Numbers. This brought up the Numbers dialog, where you could choose the number format from the pop-up menu at the top of the dialog, or type your choices manually in the fields. A sample of how your symbols will appear was at the bottom of the dialog.

Choosing Your Numbers Format OS X

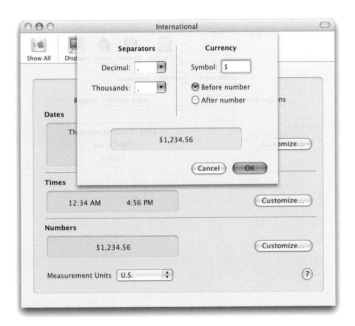

OS X: To set your numbers format in Mac OS X, click on the Apple menu and choose System Preferences. When the System Preferences pane opens, select International, then click on the Formats button. A window opens, showing your current formats for dates, times, and numbers. To change any of the formats, just click the appropriate Customize button.

new stuff:	New in the OS X version of the Numbers Preference pane is the option of choosing the Metric system as your unit of measurement. Frasier and Niles would definitely choose this option, and they'd probably choose France as their region, even though they live in Seattle.

Adjusting Your Mouse/Trackpad Speed OS 9

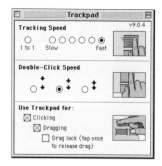

OS 9: You could control the speed of your mouse (for desktop machines) or your PowerBook/iBook trackpad through a control panel. You'd go under the Apple menu, under Control Panels, and choose Mouse (for desktop Macs) or Trackpad (for PowerBooks/iBooks).

Adjusting Your Mouse/Trackpad Speed OS X

You can control your mouse tracking speed for your desktop Mac in the Keyboard & Mouse preferences.

If you're using a PowerBook/iBook you can control your trackpad tracking speed in the Keyboard & Mouse preferences (as well as for your mouse if you have one connected).

OS X: Now, we adjust either the mouse speed (for desktop Macs) or trackpad speed (for PowerBooks/iBooks) in the same place. From the Apple menu, click on System Preferences, then select Keyboard & Mouse. Click on the Mouse button (see above left) to win tickets to Disne…no that's not right. Click on the Mouse button to set your tracking speed (how fast your cursor moves around the screen) and the speed you want your Mac to recognize that two clicks is a "double-click" (if you have a mouse with a scroll wheel, you'll also have an option for how fast you want pages to scroll). If you're using a PowerBook, you'll see a Trackpad button instead of a Mouse button (unless you have a mouse plugged into your PowerBook, in which case, you'll have a Trackpad *and* a Mouse button). Clicking on the Trackpad button brings up the options for your Trackpad.

new stuff: *If you're using Bluetooth, you're a geek. That's probably not a real surprise to the people who know you, but when they see you controlling your Mac from a keyboard that isn't plugged in or changing the song iTunes is playing on your Mac from across the room with your cellphone, you will stir up feelings in them they never knew they had—geek envy.*

Setting Your Keyboard Layout OS 9

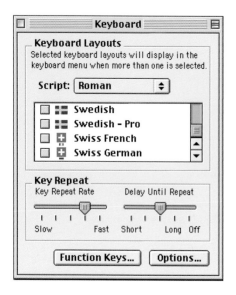

OS 9: You set the keyboard layout (depending on which language you use) by going under the Apple menu, under Control Panels, and choosing Keyboard. This brought up the dialog shown above, where you'd choose your country, and this would map the keyboard of your Mac appropriately. This was always a great starting point for pulling pranks on other people in your office while they were out at lunch.

Setting Your Keyboard Layout OS X

OS X: Now, the keyboard layout isn't part of Keyboard System Preferences at all. Instead, from the Apple menu, choose System Preferences and click on the International icon. Click on the button for Input Menu to bring up the list of keyboard layouts (as shown above). Choose as many as you like by clicking in the checkboxes. If you want to be able to access your various layouts easily, click the Show Input Menu in Menu Bar option located in the lower-left corner of the Preference pane. Now your Gujarati and Devanagari-QWERTY keyboard layouts are only one click away on the right-hand side of your menu bar.

Opening Apps Automatically at Startup OS 9

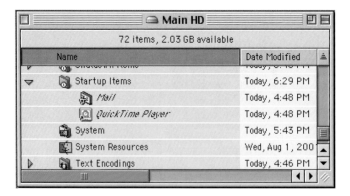

OS 9: To have a program launch automatically upon startup, you would click on its icon and make an alias of that file. Then, you'd open the System folder, find a folder named Startup Items, and place the alias there. From the next restart onward, that program (and any others with aliases in the folder) would launch automatically.

Opening Apps Automatically at Startup OS X

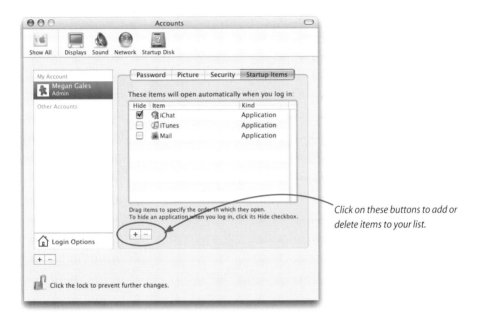

Click on these buttons to add or delete items to your list.

OS X: Now, you don't have to mess with aliases and dropping things into the System folder anymore. From the Apple menu, click on System Preferences and select Accounts. When the Preference pane opens, click on the Startup Items button to bring up a list of items that will open automatically every time you log in. To add or delete items to the list, just click on the plus or minus buttons below the application list (see above).

new stuff: *If you have several applications set to open automatically, your screen can easily get covered with open windows that you'll have to close. If you would like an item to launch at startup but remain hidden in the background, select the checkbox next to its name in the Startup Items Preference pane. You'll know the application is open from its Dock icon, but it won't clutter your desktop.*

Adjusting Your Spring-Loaded Folders OS 9

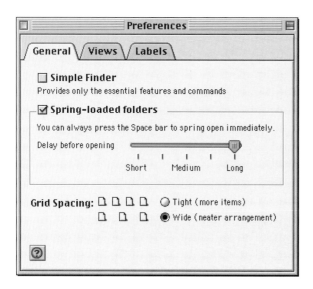

OS 9: When you dragged a file into a folder (or from one folder to another) and paused for a moment over the destination folder, it would "spring open." This kept you from double-clicking through folder after folder, and it was a very popular feature. You could control the amount of time you had to pause over a folder before it "sprang" open by going to the Edit menu on the Finder's menu bar and selecting Preferences. Clicking on the General tab brought up the dialog shown above where you could set the delay time before a folder would spring open.

Adjusting Your Spring-Loaded Folders OS X

OS X: Now, you can control how long you have to pause over a folder before it springs open by going to the Finder menu, choosing Preferences, and clicking on the General icon. You can control the amount of delay before a folder springs open using the slider (as shown above). If you want the spring-loaded feature turned off, click on the checkbox next to Spring-Loaded Folders and Windows (it's on by default). By the way, when Mac OS X first shipped, the spring-loaded folders feature wasn't in the first releases—it wasn't until Mac OS X 10.2 (Jaguar) that spring-loaded folders made their appearance. Just in case you care. You probably don't, but ya never know.

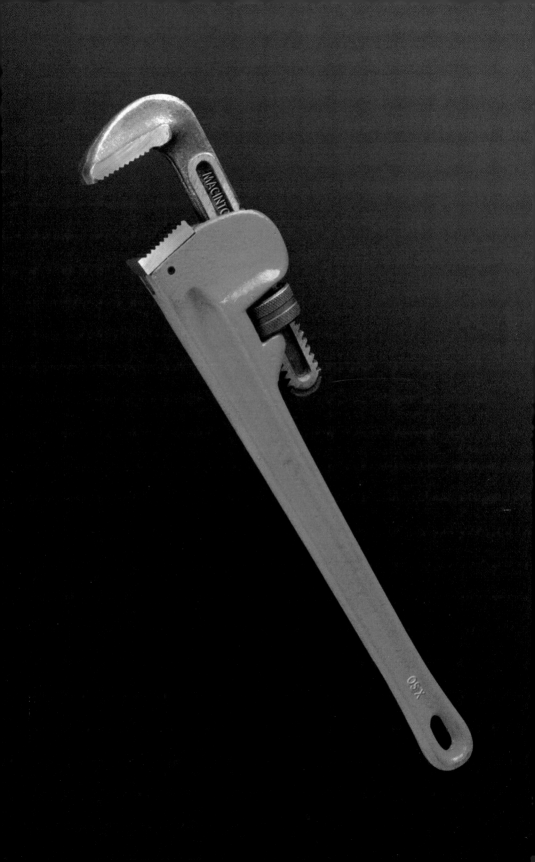

Chapter Four

If you're a Mac user, chances are you are a "creative type." Someone my father might call a "hippy," but then, he is, after all, nearly 150 years old, so I cut him some slack. For example, my dad (who is a genuinely wonderful man, and I firmly believe

Crank Up the Jams
MUSIC, PHOTOS, AND VIDEO

the father all fathers should be judged by) sadly still to this day uses the term "foxy" to describe an attractive-looking woman (he hasn't paid attention to any social vernacular since *Laugh-In* went off the air). In fact, I recently heard him call my wife "Foxy Mama" in a way that he hoped would sound complimentary. Well, my "Foxy Mama" is also a martial artist, and accordingly she beat him to a pulp. Hey, I can't say he didn't have it coming. Anyway, if you're a creative person (and I know you are), just silently pointing and clicking at text and icons isn't going to be enough for you. No, you need auditory and visual sensory stimulation. (If that sounds naughty, and it should, that makes you a bad person. Not me, mind you. Just you. Bad, bad, bad!) Well, the next time you want to play a DVD (a naughty DVD, no doubt), you'll need a little guidance on how things are done in Mac OS X (by the way, that's Mac OS "10" not "X," you sicko). That's what this chapter is all about, it's about getting music to play, video clips to run, DVDs to play, and the massive guilt you'll have from misusing these seemingly harmless tools.

Playing a Music CD OS 9

OS 9: Back in Mac OS 9, to play a music CD, you'd insert the CD in your CD-ROM drive, go under the Apple menu, and choose AppleCD Audio Player. Then when it appeared, you'd click the Play button (as shown above). In the CD Audio Player preferences, under the Edit menu, you could check the box for Autoplay to have every audio CD begin playing as soon as you inserted it.

Playing a Music CD OS X

OS X: Now, by default, when you insert a music CD, Apple's iTunes application opens. If you want to hear a certain song from the CD, when iTunes launches, you'll see a small CD icon in the Source window at the left side of the iTunes window. Clicking on it brings up a list of track names. Click on the first one you want to play and click the play arrow in the controller (top left). If you go to the iTunes menu bar and select Controls, you can set such things as Shuffle, Repeat, etc. If you want the CD to automatically play when you insert it, just go under the iTunes menu in the menu bar and choose Preferences. Click on the General icon at the top, then choose Begin Playing in the On CD Insert pop-up menu.

Pausing a CD Playing in the Background OS 9

OS 9: Back in Mac OS 9, if you were playing a music CD and wanted to pause it, you'd have to go the application menu, choose the AppleCD Audio Player to make it the active application, then click the Pause button (as shown above).

Pausing a CD Playing in the Background OS X

OS X: Now, when a CD is playing in the background, you can pause it, switch to the next track, find out the name of the track, and a host of other handy controls without leaving your current application. Just click-and-hold (or Control-click) on the iTunes icon in the Dock, and a pop-up menu of controls appears. To pause the audio CD, just choose Pause from the pop-up list.

Converting CDs to MP3 OS 9

OS 9: To convert your audio CDs to the MP3 format in Mac OS 9, you inserted your music CD into your drive and launched iTunes. You then selected the tracks you wanted to convert by clicking in the checkboxes next to their names. The final step was to click on the Import button in the top-right corner of the iTunes window.

Converting CDs to MP3 OS X

OS X: With Mac OS X, you can also convert your audio CDs to MP3 and save them on your hard drive to listen to anytime you want. Insert your audio CD, and iTunes launches. If you have an "always on" Internet connection (set in iTunes' General preferences), the track names appear in the playlist window (otherwise, it just says Track 01, Track 02, etc.). Make sure the checkboxes next to the tracks you want to convert are selected, then click on the Import button in the top-right corner of the iTunes window. iTunes saves your MP3s in the Music folder of your user account.

new stuff:	With Panther, you're not limited to just the MP3 format. You can actually choose from four different formats in the Importing preferences of iTunes. The other one that you might want to try out is the ACC format, which Apple uses for its downloads at the iTunes Music Store.

Burning Your Own Music CDs OS 9

OS 9: In Mac OS 9, if you wanted to burn a music CD, you'd open iTunes and arrange the tracks in the order you wanted them and make sure they were selected by clicking in the checkboxes by their titles. Once that was done, you inserted a blank CD and clicked the Burn CD button in the top-right corner of the iTunes window.

51915105

Burning Your Own Music CDs OS X

OS X: In Mac OS X, it works much the same—you can sort and organize music and burn your own audio CDs directly from Apple's iTunes application (shown above). Start by inserting a music CD and choosing the songs you want to burn to CD, click on the New Playlist button (the one with the big plus sign) at the bottom of the iTunes window, then drag the songs you have selected into this playlist. If you have songs you have previously ripped in your iTunes Library, drag them into this playlist as well. Arrange the songs in the order you want, then click on the Burn Disc button at the upper-right corner of the iTunes window (shown above). You'll be prompted to insert a blank CD. Once you insert it, you'll be prompted to click the Burn Disc button again and then iTunes starts burnin'.

Controlling External Speakers OS 9

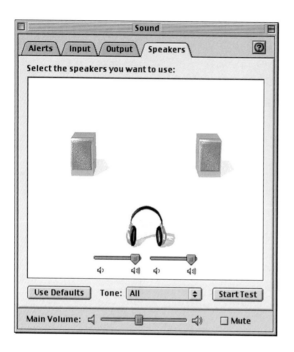

OS 9: Back in OS 9, when you wanted to control external speakers connected to your Mac, you'd go under the Apple menu, under Control Panels, and choose Sound to bring up the Sound Control Panel. Clicking on the Speakers tab opened the window shown above where you could make any adjustments you needed for your speakers (except make them sound really good).

Controlling External Speakers OS X

OS X: Now, you can control the balance, volume, and setup of external audio speakers connected to your Mac by going under the Apple menu, choosing System Preferences, and then clicking on the Sound icon to bring up the Sound preferences. When the Sound Preference pane appears, click on the Output button and simply move the Balance control to your liking.

Selecting an Audio Input Source OS 9

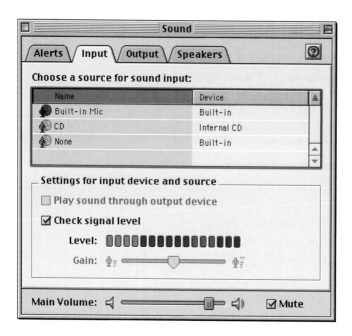

OS 9: Whenever you record audio on your Mac, you have to tell it where to "listen" for the signal. In Mac OS 9, you did this by going under the Apple menu to Control Panels and selecting Sound. When the panel opened, you clicked on the Input tab and the window pictured above opened. From here, you could select your input source (Built-in Mic, Internal CD, External Mic, etc.) and check the signal level before recording.

Selecting an Audio Input Source OS X

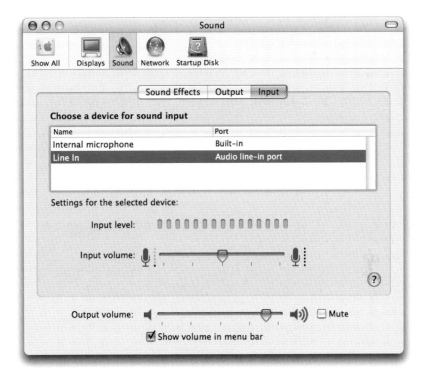

OS X: In Mac OS X, you click on the Apple menu, select System Preferences, and choose Sound. When the Sound Preference pane opens, click on the Input button and a list of available signal sources is presented. Select the desired source by clicking on its name, then adjust the signal input level with the Input Volume adjustment slider.

Recording Audio from Your Mac OS 9

OS 9: Mac OS 9 included a wonderful little application (located in the Apple Extras folder) for recording CD-quality sound called SimpleSound. The length of your recordings was limited only by the amount of available hard drive space. To use Simple-Sound, you first selected your signal input source (see page 94), chose a recording quality preset from the Sound menu, pressed Command-N to create a new file, and clicked the Record button on the SimpleSound controller (shown above). When you finished recording, you pressed the Stop button on the controller, clicked Save, and told your Mac where to save the file.

Recording Audio from Your Mac OS X

OS X: SimpleSound is gone in Mac OS X and has not been replaced with another application. If you want to do some recording, the easiest thing to do is to download a third-party application (there are plenty of them available for free or for minimal share-ware fees). There is one application on your Mac that you can use to record audio, though it's not designed specifically for that purpose. iMovie has a voice-over feature which allows you to record narration for your videos. Well, you can also record narration even if you don't have a video. Go to the Applications folder and launch iMovie. Click on the Audio button, then click the Record button (if you do not have an internal mic or have not attached an external source, it will be grayed out). When you're done recording, click the button again and save your file. Here's the crazy thing—you now have a movie file. If you want to use it as an audio file, you have to export it to another application (QuickTime, for example) and convert it to another file format. Want my advice? Download an audio application and save yourself some time and trouble.

Accessing Photos from a Digital Camera OS 9

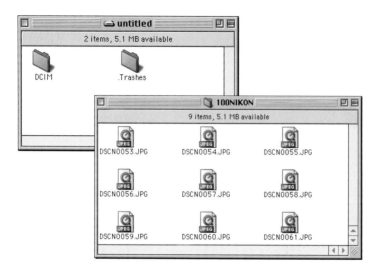

OS 9: Back in Mac OS 9, when you needed to get your digital-camera images onto your Mac, you would plug the cable that came with your camera into a USB port on your computer. In a few moments, an icon would appear on your desktop (usually named Untitled). Clicking on the icon opened a window that usually contained a folder descriptively named DCIM. You clicked on this folder, which opened yet another window containing a couple of folders, one of which had a name that bore some resemblance to the name of your camera. Clicking on this folder opened a window containing all your images labeled with names like DSCN0061, DSCN0062, DSCN0063, etc. You grabbed the ones you wanted and dragged them onto your desktop or into a folder on your hard drive.

Accessing Photos from a Digital Camera OS X

Welcome to iPhoto!
iPhoto is your best choice for importing, organizing and sharing your digital photos.
Best of all, you don't even have to download any software. Just plug in your camera.

Optimized for Mac OS X.
iPhoto was engineered to take advantage of the speed and power of
Mac OS X so you can do more with your photos, faster.

No Drivers Necessary.
iPhoto does not require any additional drivers or software, so you
can begin enjoying your digital photos the second you plug your
camera in.

So Many Ways to Share
Send photos via e-mail, print them on your home printer or create
your own professional-quality photo books. iPhoto lets you do
more with your favorite shots.

Do you want to use iPhoto when you connect your digital camera?

(Use Other)   (Decide Later) (Use iPhoto)

OS X: Now, in Mac OS X, the first time you connect (via USB or FireWire) a digital camera or memory card reader to your Mac, the window shown above opens, asking which application you would like to set as your default application for handling digital photos. The next time you hook up a camera or insert a media card, the application you selected automatically opens and downloads your photos to whatever folder you have designated. It just doesn't get much easier.

new stuff: *One of the best things about Mac OS X is the ability to use iPhoto. This amazing application is free and is packed with features that make it easy to download, catalog, view, edit, and share your digital photos.*

Taking Screen Captures OS 9

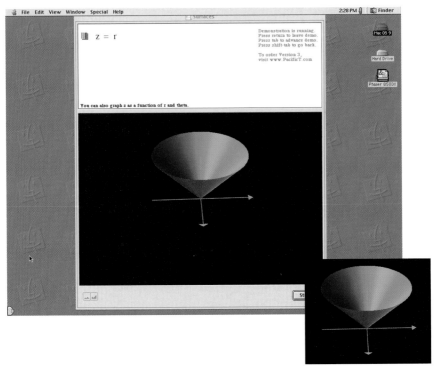

OS 9: In Mac OS 9, when you wanted to capture an image of what you were seeing on your screen, you pressed Shift-Command-3. If you wanted just a portion of the screen, the command was Shift-Command-4. This brought up a tiny crosshair that you could drag to select the portion of the screen image you wanted to capture. The capture images were saved to your desktop as .pict files.

Taking Screen Captures OS X

OS X: You can take a screen capture of the entire screen by pressing Shift-Command-3. If you want to capture an entire window that's open on your screen, press Shift-Command-4, then press the Spacebar. Your cursor changes to a little camera that you can use to click on the window you want to capture. To capture a portion of the screen, press Shift-Command-4. When your cursor changes to a crosshair, drag it to define the area you want to capture. When you release your mouse button, the capture is saved on your desktop in .pdf format.

new stuff:	Mac OS X includes a nifty little application named Grab (it's inside the Utilities folder within the Applications folder). You can use Grab to take "regular" screen captures, but it also has a timed feature that delays the capture for 10 seconds to give you time to open a window or menu that you want to capture. Grab saves the captures as .tiff files, which you can open with Preview or another application of your choosing.

Viewing Graphics Files OS 9

OS 9: Back in Mac OS 9, when you clicked on a generic graphics file (one not tied to a particular application), it would open with one of several built-in applications, depending on the file type. PictureViewer (located in the QuickTime folder) generally opened .jpg files while SimpleText opened .gif images. Once the images opened, you really had very little control over them, but it was a handy way to see an image quickly.

Viewing Graphics Files OS X

OS X: in Mac OS X, PictureViewer has been replaced by a much more powerful application—Preview. In addition to just opening files, Preview combines multiple images and allows you to preview them as thumbnails (see above). It also allows you to view your selected images as a simple slideshow. Finally, with Preview, you can export images (File>Export) to all the main graphics formats. You can open a .jpg file, for instance, and export it as a .tiff file. Very handy when you need to convert from one format to another.

Playing QuickTime Movies OS 9

OS 9: Back in Mac OS 9, to watch a QuickTime movie, all you did was double-click on the movie's icon and a QuickTime player window opened on your desktop.

Playing QuickTime Movies OS X

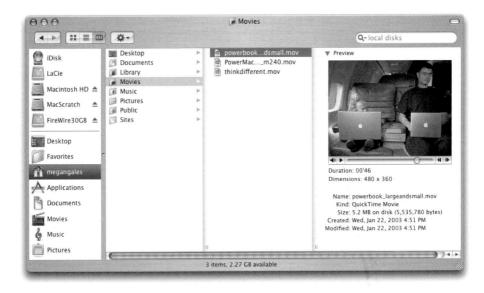

OS X: Watching QuickTime movies is really pretty much the same in Mac OS X, but a couple of new things are very convenient. If you set your window view to Column view (see page 27), you can preview movies without having to open them in QuickTime. If you have several movies and you're not sure which is the one you want to use, this is a real timesaver. Another new feature in Mac OS X is the ability to minimize a Quick-Time movie to the Dock and still have it play. Okay, it's not one of those technological breakthroughs that's going to change life as we know it—but it is pretty cool.

Watching a DVD on Your Mac OS 9

OS 9: Back in Mac OS 9, when you inserted a DVD and wanted to watch it, you'd go under the Apple menu and choose Apple DVD Player. This would bring up the round DVD Player (shown above), and you could play the DVD by clicking on the Play button in the center of the controller.

Watching a DVD on Your Mac OS X

OS X: Now, by default, Apple's DVD Player (shown above) appears automatically (after all, it figures if you inserted a DVD into your Mac, you probably want to watch it, right?). To play the DVD, just press the Play button (circled above) on the cool-looking controller. If you don't want a DVD to automatically launch when you insert it, just go under the Apple menu and choose System Preferences, then click on the CDs & DVDs icon to bring up those preferences. Then, where it says "When you insert a video DVD," choose Ignore from the pop-up menu. From then on, when you insert a DVD, your Mac will do, well…nothing—it will just ignore it and go on with its life. If you want to manually launch DVD Player, look for it in your Applications folder.

Chapter Five

 If someone walks up to you on the street and asks, "Hey, what's a display?" you'd probably answer, "Something in a store window, or perhaps on a counter to showcase a product for sale." At least

Monitors

THEY'RE CALLED DISPLAYS IN MAC OS X

that's the kind of answer you'd give if you worked for an ad agency. Now, let's ask a regular person. I'll go ask Sarah Hughes, our company's staff writer and head of PR. Why Sarah? Because Sarah's desk is probably the closest to mine, and I can see from here that she's at her desk. Just a moment while I go and ask her, "What's a display?" I'll be right back. Okay, you're not going to believe this. Sarah said (and I swear this is true), "It's something set up to showcase products." However, truth be told, I think Sarah once worked for an ad agency, so her answer may have been skewed. So, if that's the definition of a display, what's the definition of a monitor? Sarah has now left her desk, so I'll have to go over to Dave's desk (also close by) to ask him the question, "What's a monitor?" I'll be right back. Okay, as expected, Dave said, "It's a computer monitor." It's pretty clear to everyone (meaning at least Dave and me) that the word "display" means "something in a store" and the word "monitor" means "computer monitor." But if a rose by any other name would smell as sweet, a monitor called a display is still as bright. I have a theory about why Apple calls monitors displays: It's all part of a plot to get you into the Apple stores (found at pricier malls) by using the psychological camouflage of the word "display." Hey, it's not that far-fetched.

Setting Monitor Brightness OS 9

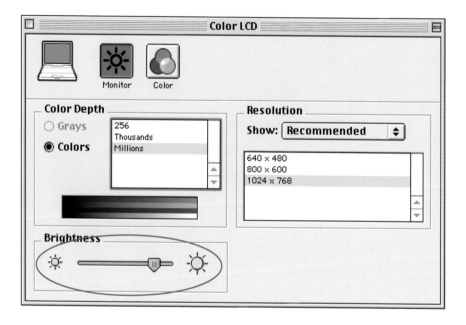

Back in Mac OS 9, to set the brightness of your monitor, you would go under the Apple menu, to Control Panels, and choose Monitors. This brought up the Control Panel shown above, and at the bottom left-hand corner was a slider for controlling the overall brightness of your monitor.

Setting Display Brightness OS X

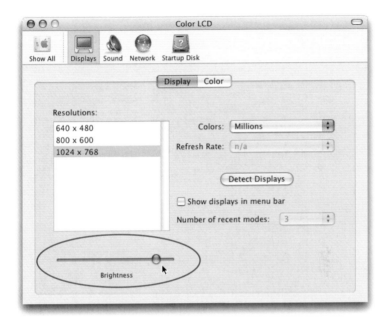

OS X: Now, you set the overall brightness for your display (monitor) by going under the Apple menu and choosing System Preferences. In the System Preferences window, click on the icon for Displays. When the Displays Preference pane appears, use the Brightness slider in the lower left-hand corner to adjust overall brightness (as shown).

Choosing Your Monitor's Resolution OS 9

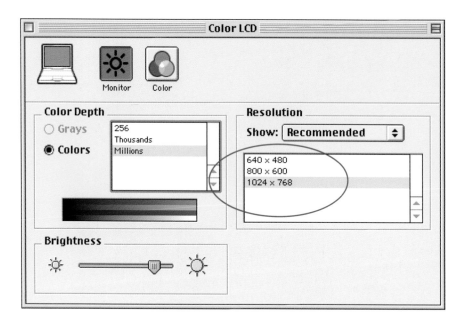

OS 9: Back in Mac OS 9, to change the resolution of your Mac's monitor, you'd go under the Apple menu, to the Control Panels folder, and choose Monitor. When the Monitor Control Panel opened, you'd choose your desired resolution from the list of available resolutions. (Your choices are limited by the size of your monitor, and the available video RAM installed on your Mac.)

Choosing Your Display's Resolution OS X

OS X: Now, to choose the resolution for your display, you go under the Apple menu, launch System Preferences, and click on the Displays icon to bring up the pane shown above. Click on the Display button, and choose your desired resolution from the list on the left side of the pane. You can choose any resolution that isn't "grayed" out.

new stuff: *If you have the Show Displays in Menu Bar checkbox turned on, you'll also be able to choose your resolution setting from the menu bar at the top-right corner of your screen. You can open the Displays Preferences pane from there as well.*

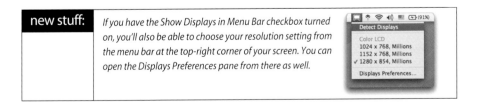

Choosing Thousands or Millions of Colors OS 9

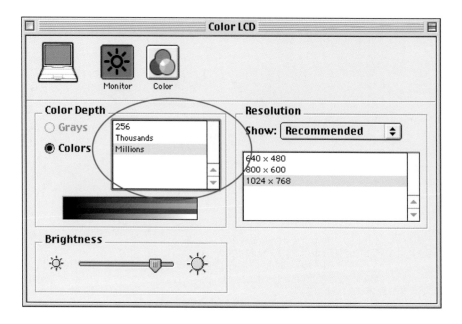

OS 9: To choose how many colors your monitor would display back in Mac OS 9, you'd go under the Apple menu, to the Control Panels folder, and choose Monitor. When the Monitor Control Panel opened, you'd choose how many colors to display. *Note:* One reason to lower the number of colors displayed was to increase performance.

Choosing Thousands or Millions of Colors OS X

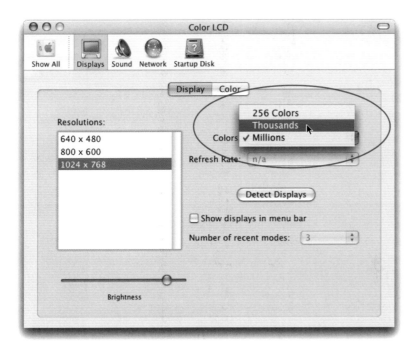

OS X: Now, you go under the Apple menu and choose System Preferences. Click on the Display icon to bring up the Displays Preference pane. There's a pop-up list of color choices in the upper right-hand corner of the pane (as shown above). Just choose the one you want and close the pane.

Using Two Monitors OS 9

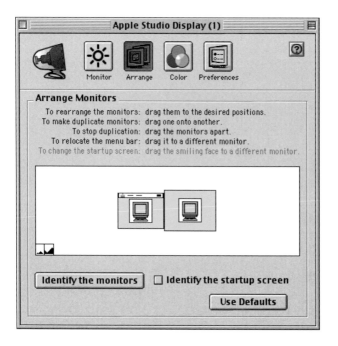

OS 9: If you have a video card capable of supporting two monitors, Mac OS 9 gave you the ability to either mirror the two displays (both would have the same image) or to arrange them to function like one big monitor. Mirroring was good for things like running a video projector because it allowed you to see the same image on your screen as the projector was displaying. Arranging the displays side-by-side (as shown above in the Monitor Control Panel) created a bigger desktop workspace.

Using Two Displays OS X

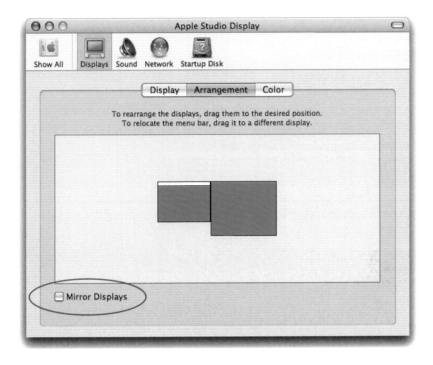

OS X: If your Mac is capable of supporting multiple displays (you may need to install a second graphics card), go under the Apple menu and choose System Preferences. Click on the Displays icon to open the Displays Preference pane, then click the Arrangement button (not visible if you have only one display). This is where you can choose how you want the displays to function. If you want both displays to have the same image, check the box to turn on Mirror Displays. With some Macs, it may be necessary to put the computer to sleep and wake it up before it detects the second display (or click on the Detect Displays button that appears in the Display pane). You shouldn't have to do a restart, however.

Putting Your Monitor to Sleep OS 9

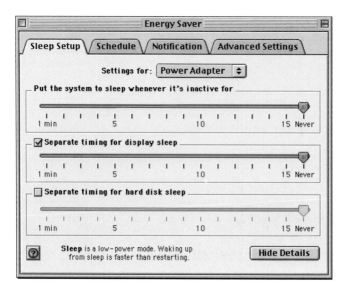

OS 9: In Mac OS 9, when you wanted to set your monitor to go to sleep after a period of inactivity, you went to the Apple menu, to Control Panels, and chose Energy Saver. This brought up a dialog with a single Energy Use slider. To configure the settings for your display, you clicked on the Show Details button in the lower-right corner. This brought up the big dialog pictured above, which allowed you to set separate sleep settings for your entire system, monitor, and hard drive.

Putting Your Display to Sleep OS X

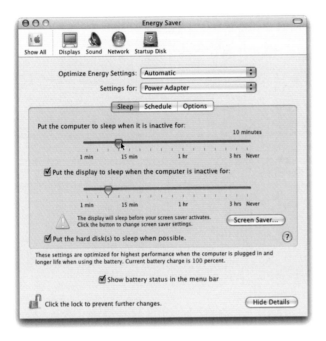

OS X: Now, to put your display to sleep to save battery and/or extend the life of your display, you go under the Apple menu and choose System Preferences. Then, click on the Energy Saver icon to bring up the Energy Saver Preference pane. Click on the Sleep button, then click the Put the Display to Sleep when the Computer Is Inactive For checkbox. Use the slider just below the checkbox (as shown above) to choose the delay before your display goes to sleep. If you want to set your Mac to turn itself on every day (don't even go there), click on the Schedule button and set the days and times for Start Up and Shut Down.

new stuff:	If you're using a PowerBook, there's a checkbox at the bottom of the Energy Saver Preference pane that adds an item to your menu bar that lets you see how much battery life is left. If you click-and-hold on this menu item, you can choose to open the Energy Saver Preference pane. Mighty handy.	

Choosing Your Monitor Profile OS 9

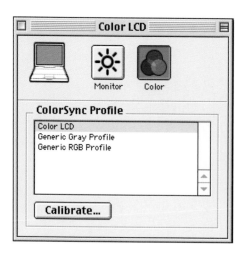

OS 9: Back in Mac OS 9, you chose your monitor color profile by going under the Apple menu, into the Control Panels folder, and choosing Monitors to bring up the dialog shown above. Clicking on the button labeled Color brought up a list of installed profiles to pick from.

Choosing Your Display Profile OS X

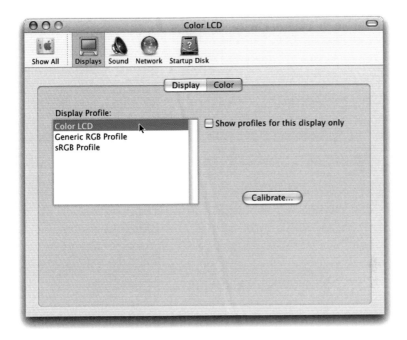

OS X: Now, you go under the Apple menu, choose System Preferences, and click on the Displays icon. In the Displays Preference pane, click on the Color button to bring up the pane shown above. Choose the profile appropriate for your display from the list of built-in profiles (as shown).

Calibrating Your Monitor OS 9

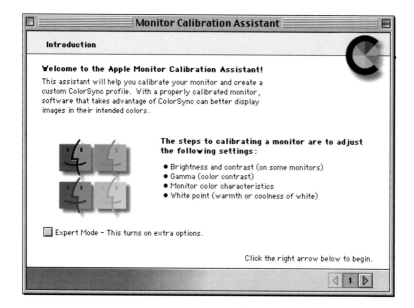

OS 9: Back in Mac OS 9, to calibrate your monitor, you'd go to the Apple menu, open Control Panels, and choose Monitors. When the dialog opened, you clicked on the Color button to bring up a list of monitor profiles, then clicked the Calibrate button at the bottom of the dialog. This brought up the Monitor Calibration Assistant (pictured above), which walked you through the steps to calibrate your monitor.

Calibrating Your Display OS X

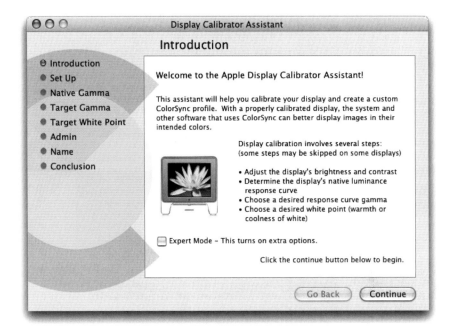

OS X: Now, to calibrate your display, you go under the Apple menu and choose System Preferences. In the System Preferences window, click on the Displays icon to bring up the Displays Preference pane. When it opens, click on the Color button. In the Color pane, click on the Calibrate button, and the Display Calibrator Assistant (shown above) appears and leads you through the step-by-step process of calibrating your display.

Chapter Six

Okay, why did I put printing and fonts together in the same chapter? Is it because these two have so much in common, or is it because these are two incredibly boring subjects? (Hint: It's fonts and printing.

Fonts and Printing
PERHAPS NOT THE MOST FUN CHAPTER

What do you think?) Hey, this isn't as bad as what I originally had planned for this chapter, which was facial exfoliation and printing. See, *now* printing sounds like fun. Luckily, in Mac OS X, printing is about the easiest it's ever been. In fact, I doubt there's ever been a platform in the history of computers whose printing setup has been easier and more intuitive than Mac OS X's. For example, when I wanted to connect my Mac to a network printer, I just called Brian (our in-house IT); he came to my office and messed with some cables and dialogs while I went out to lunch. When I came back, son-of-a-gun, the whole thing was up and running—and I could access all our printers. See, that's pretty easy, and that's what this chapter is all about—the easy way to print and install fonts in Mac OS X, like you used to do in Mac OS 9. For example, back in OS 9, there was no Brian. He didn't work for us, so I had to do everything myself. I was down on the ground, behind my G4, plugging in cables (and cussing), but it wasn't long after the launch of Mac OS X that we hired Brian, and since then, printing has become much easier. Coincidence? I think not.

Installing Fonts OS 9

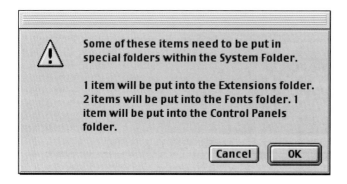

OS 9: In Mac OS 9, when you wanted to install fonts, all you had to do was select the font(s) you wanted to install, drag them on top of the System Folder, and drop them in. A dialog popped up, letting you know that the fonts were going to be put in the Fonts folder. It was pretty much a no-brainer.

Installing Fonts OS X

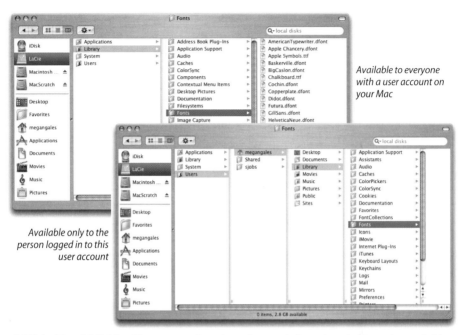

Available to everyone with a user account on your Mac

Available only to the person logged in to this user account

OS X: In Mac OS X, it's still as easy as just dragging-and-dropping the fonts into a folder; the only tricky part is which folder, because there's more than one Fonts folder. If you're the only person who uses your Mac, you can drop them in the Fonts folder that appears inside the Library folder. You can also install fonts here if you share your Mac with other people, and you want these other people to all have access to these fonts. However, if you share your Mac with other users and want your own separate fonts (in other words, you're stingy and don't want to share), then instead you'd drag-and-drop your fonts into a different place. Go to your Users folder, then to your individual Home folder, then look in the Library folder (that's inside your Home folder) for a folder named Fonts. Drop 'em in there, and then these fonts will be available only to you when you log in.

new stuff:	Didn't you hate it in Mac OS 9 when you had to quit an application before it could use the font you just installed? With Mac OS X, any fonts you install are available to use immediately—even for applications that are already running.

Organizing Fonts OS 9

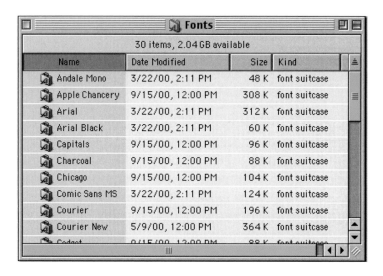

OS 9: In Mac OS 9, there really wasn't much you could do to organize your fonts other than sorting them by name, kind, etc.

Organizing Fonts OS X

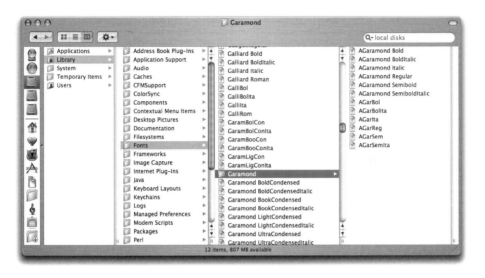

OS X: One feature of Mac OS X that helps with font organization is the ability to keep fonts together in folders within the Fonts folder. That doesn't sound like such a big deal, but if you tried it in Mac OS 9, the system would not recognize them. It would look in the Fonts folder, see your neatly organized folders and say, "Hey—these aren't fonts, they're folders. What do you expect me to do with folders?" Mac OS X understands your need for organization. If it looks in the Fonts folder and sees another folder, it looks in it and opens any fonts it finds. Don't push it, though. It will only look one level deep.

new stuff:	*Mac OS X provides basic font management through the Font panel and Font Book (for more on Font Book, check out Chapter Eleven). In Mac OS X-native applications (also known as Cocoa apps), such as TextEdit, you can access the Font panel from the Format menu item (on the app's menu bar) or by pressing Command-T. It's limited (hey, it's free!), but does give you the ability to make font collections, preview typefaces, and see all the characters available for a font. Note: If you don't see the Collections column in the Font panel, drag out the bottom-right corner until you can see it.*

Selecting a Printer OS 9

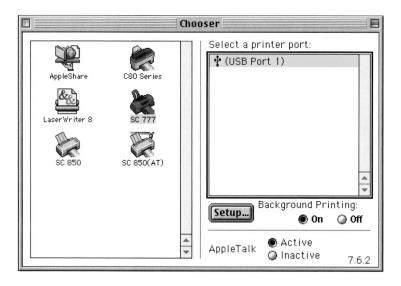

OS 9: Designating a printer was something you seemed to have to do often in Mac OS 9. Fortunately, it was easy. You just went to the Apple menu and selected Chooser. When the Chooser dialog opened (pictured above), you clicked on the icon for the printer you wanted to use. It wasn't hard, but it was a pain because you had to do this every time you wanted to use a different printer.

Selecting a Printer OS X

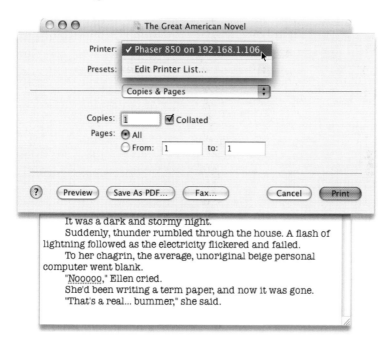

OS X: In Mac OS X, when you tell a document to print, the Print dialog opens. At the top is a pop-up menu showing the name of the currently selected printer. If that's the one you want to use, click the Print button. To select a different printer, click on the pop-up menu and choose the one you want from the list that opens. Don't see the one you want? Select Edit Printer List and add the printer you want to use (see page 133). If you're a speed freak, the next time you're printing something, click on the printer icon that appears in the Dock and choose Keep in Dock from the pop-up menu, then you can drag-and-drop documents directly to the printer icon (see below).

new stuff:	When Mac OS X was first released, Apple had done away with Desktop Printers. Well, they're back in Panther. To create a Desktop Printer, in the Printer List of the Printer Setup Utility, click on a printer to highlight it, and then go to Printers in the menu bar and choose Create Desktop Printer. This creates a desktop icon that you can use to drag-and-drop documents onto that you want to quickly print. Or you can double-click on the icon to monitor currently printing documents.

Adding a Printer OS 9

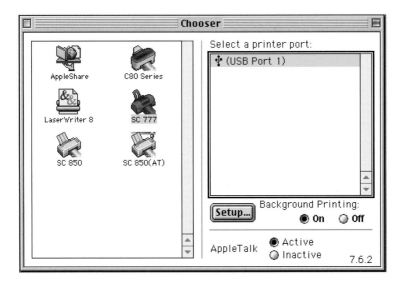

OS 9: In Mac OS 9, you could add as many printers as you liked by installing the drivers provided by the manufacturer. You could always tell which drivers were installed by going to the Apple menu and selecting the Chooser. If a printer's icon was visible in the Chooser, its driver was installed.

Adding a Printer OS X

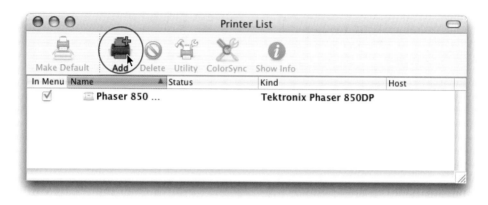

OS X: Adding printers in Mac OS X is pretty much the same except that it comes with a ton of drivers already installed. Before you go to the trouble of downloading and installing a driver for your printer, just connect it to your Mac and try printing a document. Chances are pretty good that it will just work. What a concept! From any application, press Command-P to bring up the print dialog. Click on the Printer pop-up menu and select Edit Printers List. When the list of current printers opens, click on the Add icon (shown above). In the dialog that appears, click on the pop-up menu at the top and you'll see a list of the ways a printer can be connected to your Mac. If you're using your basic inkjet, odds are it's hooked up to one of your USB ports. Select one of the connection options and choose your printer from the list that opens.

new stuff:	If hard drive space is an issue for you and you want to get rid of the printer drivers you don't anticipate needing, go to the main Library and locate a folder named Printers. Open it up and locate the drivers you want to keep. Select all the others and drag them to the Trash (or hit Command-Delete). I just did that on this iBook and got rid of 218.7 MB!

Sharing a Printer OS 9

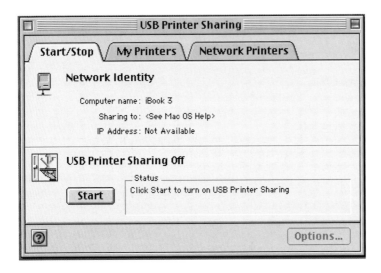

OS 9: In order to share a printer connected to your Mac with other people on your network, you went to the Apple menu, to Control Panels, and opened USB Printer Sharing. Once it was open, you clicked on the Start button in the lower section of the window. You also had to install a driver for your printer that allowed it to be accessed over a network.

Sharing a Printer OS X

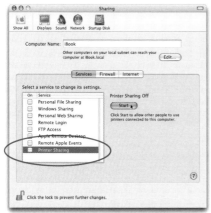

Sharing preferences

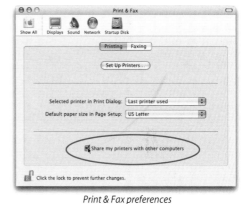

Print & Fax preferences

OS X: In Mac OS X, you have a couple of options for setting your Mac to share its printer. The first is done in the Sharing Preference pane. From the Apple menu, click on System Preferences and choose Sharing. When the pane pictured above (left) opens, click on the Printer Sharing checkbox at the bottom left of the list. If AppleTalk is not active, you'll need to enable it before your printer can be shared (see page 137). Here's another way to share your printer: Instead of opening the Sharing Preference pane, open the Print & Fax preferences. The window shown above (right) opens. All you have to do is click the Share My Printers with Other Computers checkbox. Why would you do it one way as opposed to another? Beats me.

Making AppleTalk Active OS 9

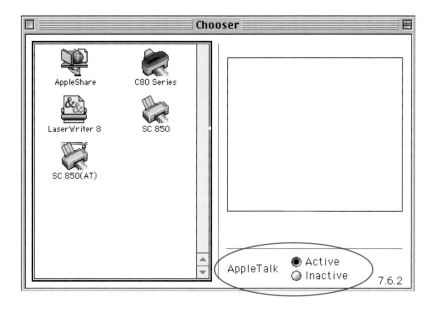

OS 9: To activate AppleTalk back in OS 9, you'd go under the Apple menu and select Chooser. In the lower-right corner of the Chooser window were two buttons enabling you to make AppleTalk active or inactive.

Making AppleTalk Active OS X

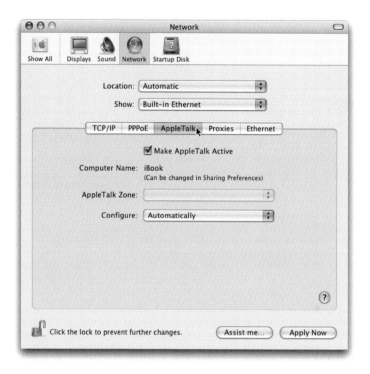

OS X: In Mac OS X, the only thing you need AppleTalk for is to share a printer that's connected to another computer on your network (as opposed to being connected to the network directly). To enable AppleTalk, from the Apple menu, choose System Preferences. When the System Preferences pane appears, click on the Network icon. Click on the AppleTalk button (as shown above), then click the checkbox labeled Make AppleTalk Active (near the top of the pane).

Viewing the Print Queue OS 9

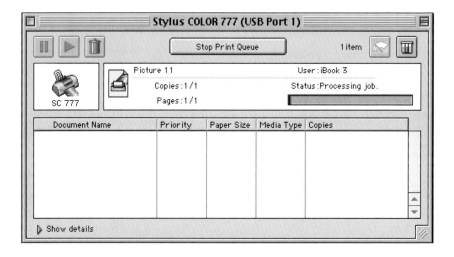

OS 9: In Mac OS 9, every time you told a document to print, the OS secretly launched an application called Print Monitor. The document spooled to the Print Monitor, which then sent it to whatever printer was selected. If you wanted to see what was in the print queue or changed your mind and wanted to stop the presses, you clicked on the active applications menu (top-right corner of your screen) and chose Print Monitor. If you were really fast and got it opened before your document was sent to the printer, you had the opportunity to cancel, rearrange, or hold until a specific time.

Viewing the Print Queue OS X

OS X: In Mac OS X, when you tell a document to print, you see an icon for your printer appear in the Dock—no sneaking around here, you can see your printer right on your Dock. That's the only way you'll know it's running because it won't open a window and take over your screen. If you want to see the print queue, however, simply click on the printer's icon in the dock and a window opens, showing you a list of all current printing activity.

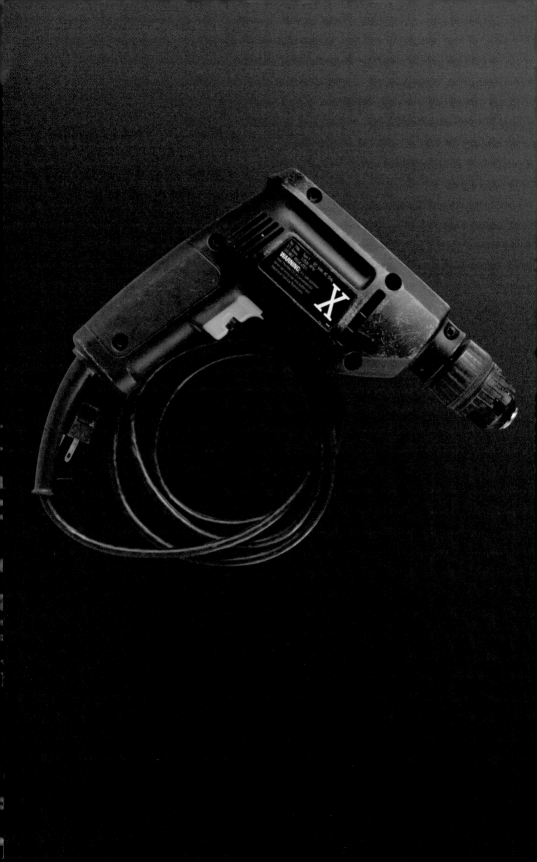

Chapter Seven

I know why you came to this chapter. You're looking for fun, aren't you? And you know down deep in your soul that when it comes to sheer unadulterated fun, there's nothing like a chapter on networking.

Networking and the Internet
HOW COULD THIS BE ANYTHING BUT A PARTY?

It's kind of like a *Macs Gone Wild on Spring Break* video (only without the video, or spring break, or anything even remotely wild). Admittedly, a chapter on networking would be almost as boring as a chapter on printing and fonts (don't worry, I would never write a boring chapter like printing and fonts, so whatever you do, don't look at Chapter Six). Anyway, since I knew I was going to have to cover networking, I thought I'd better find a more exciting topic to go with it to help offset the innate boringness of networking. *(Note to Editor: If "boringness" isn't actually a word, use "boralating" instead.)* So, in short, I added the flashy, exciting, Vegas-a-go-go world of the Internet to this boring networking chapter. This creates what will go down in history as a brilliant marriage of two polar opposite topics to create a "swingin' über-chapter," or it could turn out to be a topic-ganging calamity that shall bear the eternal mark of shame. *(Whispered: Little do they know that the Internet part of this chapter may actually eclipse the networking part in terms of "boring info per square inch" because the Internet part is about TCP/IP settings, IP addresses, etc., and there's little or no mention of Vegas. Of course, I would never admit to that, because it might hurt book sales.)*

Sharing Your Mac with Other Users OS 9

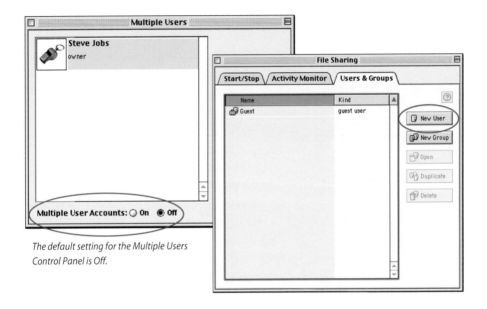

The default setting for the Multiple Users Control Panel is Off.

OS 9: In Mac OS 9, you had the ability to set up user accounts on your Mac by going to the Control Panels and opening Multiple Users. After clicking the On button, you opened the File Sharing Control Panel, clicked on the Users & Groups tab, and added the new users.

Sharing Your Mac with Other Users OS X

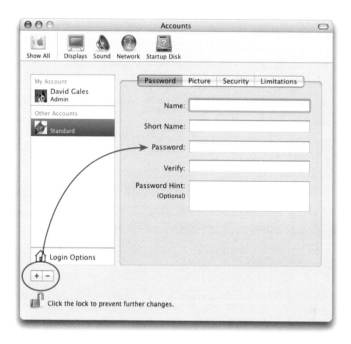

OS X: In Mac OS X, to add a user, go to the Apple menu to System Preferences and click on Accounts. The pane opens and you see a list of current users to the left. To add a new user, click the "+" button at the bottom of the window and fill in the new user's information. One very important decision you need to make is whether you want this user to have administrative privileges (add/delete users, change passwords, etc.). If so, click the Security button and check the Allow User to Administer this Computer box at the bottom of the window. You can set limits and privileges for users who are not administrators by clicking the Limitations button and setting the various options

new stuff:	If you're a CIA wannabe or just want to keep nosy people from reading your files, Mac OS X includes the FileVault. You can set your Mac to encrypt and decrypt your Home folder on the fly. All you have to do is remember your password if you ever want to see your files again.	

Setting User Privileges OS 9

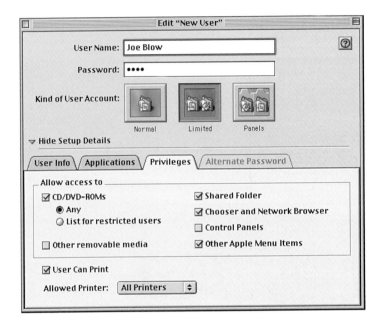

OS 9: In Mac OS 9, if you wanted someone to be able to use your Mac, but didn't want to give him carte blanche, you could assign privileges. This could be as general as "Cannot use CD drive" or as specific as which applications he was allowed to use. To set the privileges, you went to the Apple menu, selected Control Panels, and clicked on Users & Groups. When the dialog opened and you selected a user, the window shown above opened and you could set the options however you desired.

Setting User Privileges OS X

OS X: In Mac OS X, you can assign privileges for any user who is not an administrator. From the Apple menu, select System Preferences, and choose Accounts. When the list of users appears, select one and click the Limitations button (not visible if the user has administrative privileges). From the window that opens, you can set that user's privileges. You might think that if you're not in an office environment you wouldn't have much use for this feature. Watch your four-year-old clicking and dragging stuff all over the desktop someday and you'll realize it might not be such a bad idea.

Controlling Access OS 9

OS 9: In Mac OS 9, if you wanted to control access to certain areas of your computer (as opposed to setting privileges for individual users), you could set up groups and set the level of access for the entire group. This was a lot easier than having to do it for every user. You could, for instance, have groups for Marketing, Accounting, Sales, etc. Any user who was in the Sales group would have whatever privileges were assigned to that group. Users could be in more than one group, but did not have to be in any group. It got pretty complicated. It also didn't protect any of your personal files, and it was pretty easy for other users in your group to modify or delete them.

Controlling Access OS X

OS X: Access to files in Mac OS X is controlled in large part by where the files are stored. Files saved in certain areas (the main Library and System folder, for example) are accessible only to persons having administrator privileges. There are areas that can be accessed by anyone on a network and areas open to anyone who has an account on a particular Mac. Then, there are user accounts—accessible only to the owner (and anyone with whom they have shared their login information). Fully explaining user accounts is way beyond the scope of this book, but it's something you'll want to get at least a basic understanding of. It can be a bit confusing at first (especially when you try to delete a file and are told you don't have sufficient permission), but once you understand the big picture, you'll appreciate how easy it is to keep your files safe and private.

Sharing Your Files OS 9

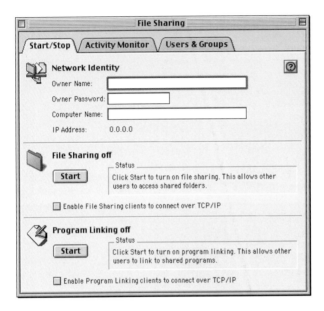

OS 9: In Mac OS 9, to share files on your Mac with other users on your network, you went to the Apple menu, selected Control Panels, and chose File Sharing. After entering the Network Identity information, you clicked the Start button.

Sharing Your Files OS X

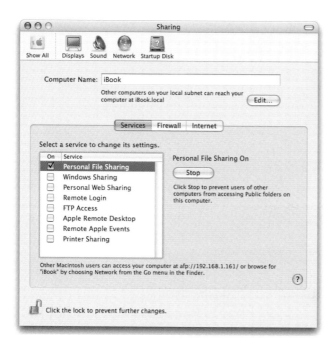

OS X: In Mac OS X, from the Apple menu, select System Preferences, and choose Sharing. When the Sharing Preference pane (shown above) opens, click in the box next to Personal File Sharing. Your Mac now shows up on the network so that others can access it. Of course, they'll only have access to the areas you have specified (see "Setting User Privileges" on page 145).

---

new stuff:	If a person on your network needs to send you a file, but doesn't have an account on your Mac, they can connect as a guest. The only thing they'll be able to do as a guest is drop files in your Drop Box, but if you want them to be able to do more, you have to give them an account—right? You can access your Drop Box by going to your Home directory and clicking on the Public folder.

Connecting to a Network: Configuring OS 9

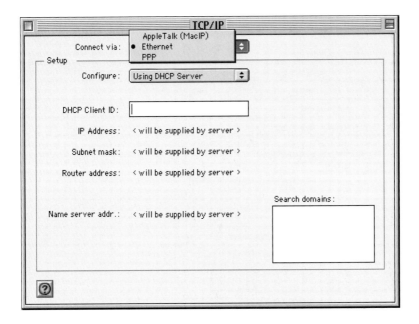

OS 9: Two steps were involved in the process of configuring your Mac for connecting to a network in Mac OS 9. The first step was to open the TCP/IP Control Panel and enter your IP address and DNS server information. The second step was to open the AppleTalk Control Panel and select the type of network you were connecting to: Ethernet, LocalTalk, or AirPort (if you were connecting to an AirPort network, you had to open the AirPort Control Panel and configure it as well). An additional third step was sometimes part of the network configuration process in Mac OS 9—cussing more times than you usually do during 18 holes of golf when you couldn't connect to the network after setting everything up.

Connecting to a Network: Configuring OS X

OS X: In Mac OS X, you only need to open one preference to configure your network (two if you're going wireless; see page 155). From the Apple menu, select System Preferences, click on Network, and the Preference pane shown above opens. If you had already configured your network settings in Mac OS 9, you'll see that Mac OS X has taken the liberty of entering the information already. Erase it! What an insult. You're no wimpy, lightweight computer user—but you're no fool, either, so if the information's correct, leave it alone. If the information is not already entered, contact your network administrator or Internet Service Provider and ask them for the information, then enter it manually. If you're going to be connecting to Macs that are not using Mac OS X, you need to enable AppleTalk by clicking on its button and selecting the appropriate checkbox in the window that opens.

Connecting to a Network OS 9

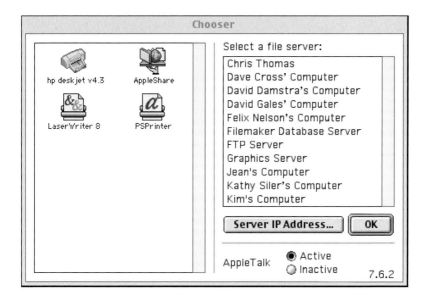

OS 9: To connect to a local network in Mac OS 9, you went to the Apple menu and selected Chooser. When the Chooser opened (assuming you had configured your network settings), you saw an icon for AppleShare. Clicking on this icon brought up a list of any computers currently available. You selected the one you wanted, entered any user information and password, and you were connected.

Connecting to a Network OS X

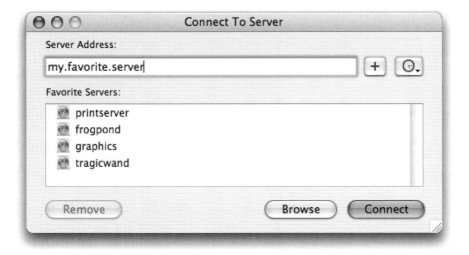

OS X: Since there is no Chooser in Mac OS X, to connect to a network, you go to the Finder's menu bar, click on Go, and select Connect to Server from the drop-down menu (or use the keyboard shortcut Command-K for...Konnect?). The window shown above opens and you see a list of any servers you have marked as favorites. If you don't have any favorites, you can enter an address in the box at the top of the window or click the Browse button to see a list of all computers available.

AirPort: Going Wireless OS 9

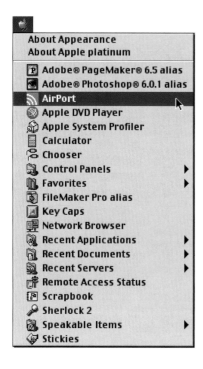

OS 9: Back in OS 9, you'd turn on AirPort wireless access by going under the Apple menu, and right at the top was AirPort. You'd click on it, and it would open the AirPort Control Panel.

AirPort: Going Wireless OS X

OS X: Now, you can access AirPort from the System Preferences, but there's a better way if you use AirPort a lot. You have to set it up (just once) by going under the Apple menu and choosing System Preferences. When the System Preferences panel appears, click on the Network icon, then where it says "Show," choose AirPort from the pop-up menu. (Note: If you don't have an AirPort card installed, AirPort won't be one of the choices.) Then, click on the AirPort button, and at the bottom of the AirPort panel is a checkbox to Show Airport Status in Menu Bar. Turn this checkbox on, and you'll be able to turn AirPort on/off, access various networks, and even open the preferences by clicking-and-holding on the icon in the menu bar.

Setting Internet Preferences OS 9

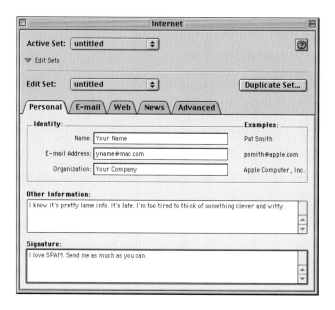

OS 9: To set up your Mac to be able to connect to the Internet in Mac OS 9, you opened the Control Panels from the Apple menu and chose the Internet Control Panel. The somewhat-confusing dialog shown above opened and allowed you to enter information for your e-mail account and other online services.

Getting Ready to Go Online OS X

OS X: If you haven't already configured your network preferences, you need to do that first by going to the Apple menu, selecting System Preferences, and choosing Network (see page 151). The Network Preference pane shows your current networks and its status. A green icon means the network is active and ready for you to go online. If the icon is red, click on it to highlight the network and then click the Configure button. Cable and DSL modems use the built-in Ethernet and dial-up uses the internal modem. Once you're in the right Preference pane, enter the information provided by your Internet Service Provider, such as the access phone number for dial-up, your user name, and your password.

new stuff:	You probably noticed the .Mac icon in the System Preferences. This is the new online service rolled out by Apple that has a plethora of features and services. There are some handy features, so it's worth checking out. Just click the Sign Up button in the lower-right corner of the .Mac Preference pane to connect to the .mac site and get more information.

Setting Up Your Modem OS 9

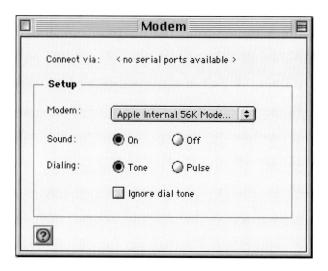

OS 9: Before you could connect to a network with your modem in Mac OS 9, you had to set your modem preferences. To do that, you went under the Apple menu to Control Panels, and selected Modem. The window shown above opened and you selected your modem from the drop-down list, set the sound and dialing options, and decided to require or ignore a dial tone.

Setting Up Your Modem OS X

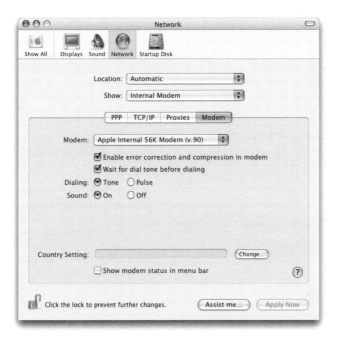

OS X: The modem preferences in Mac OS X are accessed from the Network Preference pane. From the Apple menu, select System Preferences, and choose Network.
When the pane opens, click on the drop-down menu labeled Show and select Internal
Modem. Click on the Modem button, choose your modem from the drop-down menu
at the top, and then set your other options.

Searching on the Internet OS 9

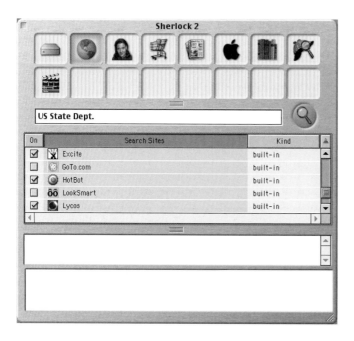

OS 9: In OS 9, you could use Sherlock 2 (the built-in Find function) to search the Internet as long as you had an active Internet connection. You'd just press Command-F to bring up Sherlock 2, then you'd click one of the icons across the top (except the first one, your hard drive) and you could do a basic search (using some of the popular Web search engines), or you could search for people, shop for items, news, search Apple's Web site, dictionary, movie times, and even create your own custom search channels.

Searching on the Internet OS X

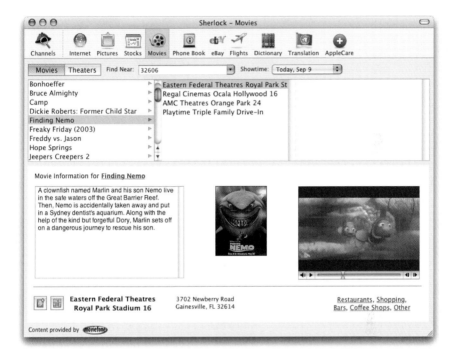

OS X: Now, Sherlock is exclusively for searching the Web, and it no longer performs searches of your hard drive or local disks. Again, you click on the icon for the type of search you want to perform, type in your search term, then hit the search button. Why would you use this instead of one of the regular online search engines? You wouldn't for most things, but if you're looking for movie times, for instance, Sherlock rocks. Once it knows your zip code, it brings up every movie at every theater in your area. Click on the one you're thinking about, and a short description and a QuickTime trailer pop up. How cool is that?

Chapter Eight

Now, where would you put stuff that really didn't fit into the other categories? That's right, into a miscellaneous chapter, but I'm not a big fan of the word "miscellaneous." I even prefer the shorter "misc.," especially

Other Stuff

THE LAND OF LITTLE LOST COMMANDS

since there's a reasonable chance that I'll misspell miscellaneous most of the time; so I switched the chapter title to "Other Stuff." I know what you're thinking— "…but Scott, you've got a spell checker, right?" While it's true that I have a spell checker, I seldom use it. Why? Because I have editors. Not just one editor mind you, multiple editors, and it's their job to (a) check my spelling manually, and (b) make me sound significantly smarter than I am (for example, originally I didn't use the words "significantly smarter," I used the words "more smartest"). However, while you're reading this, you're probably thinking, "Ya know, Scott really doesn't sound all that smart." That's simply because I don't pay my editors enough. Why don't I pay them more (you might ask)? It's because they're stealing from me. Constantly. For example, I'll go into my office on a particular day, and my pen will be missing. Of course, I go straight to my editors and announce, "Hey, my pen's missing," and they all get this look on their face like, "We didn't take it." But that goes against the ingrained nature of all editors, which is to lie when asked a direct question. Here's proof: I asked them, "Hey, how'd you like the intro copy for the Other Stuff chapter?" and they said, "Great! Nice job. You've done it again." Clearly, they can't be trusted.

Ejecting a Disk OS 9

OS 9: Back in Mac OS 9, to eject a disk (an external hard drive, CD, Zip disk, etc.), you'd click on the icon of the disk you wanted to eject and either drag it to the Trash, or you would press Command-Y (the shortcut for Put Away). You could also choose Eject from the Special menu, but that feels so 1980s.

Ejecting a Disk OS X

OS X: The easiest way to eject a disk is to press the Eject key on your keyboard. If your keyboard doesn't have an Eject key, try holding down the F12 key. Need another option? Click on the disk's icon and drag it to the Trash. The Trash icon immediately changes to an Eject symbol (which mentally feels better than dragging a perfectly good disk into the Trash), and the disk is ejected as soon as you drop it on the Eject, icon. You can also click on the disk's icon and go to the menu bar, select File, and click on Eject. The keyboard shortcut for this is Command-E for Eject (much better than Command-Y, as in "Y in the world was Command-Y the shortcut for ejecting a disk?"). One more option for ejecting a disk—Control-click on the disk icon and select Eject from the contextual menu.

new stuff: *Panther has added yet another way to eject a disk that may be even faster than the ways mentioned above. When you're in a Finder window, you'll see a little Eject icon next to each mounted disk at the top of the Sidebar. Just click on the icon and the disk ejects.*

Removing an Item from the Apple Menu OS 9

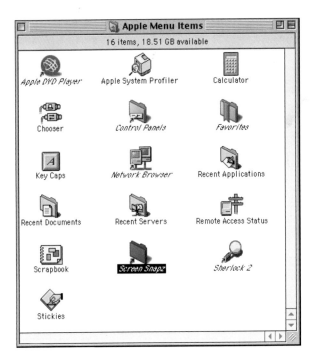

OS 9: To remove an item from the Apple menu in Mac OS 9, you had to go to the System Folder, into the Apple Menu Items folder, and drag the item outside the folder (as shown above).

Removing an Item from the Dock OS X

OS X: In Mac OS X, to remove an item from the Dock, just click on the Dock icon and drag it right out of the Dock. An animated puff of smoke appears to let you know it's removed. If you drag an item out and it snaps right back, it's either an open application or a document window that you've minimized (see Chapter Two). If it's an application, click-and-hold on its Dock icon and select Quit from the contextual menu. Once the application quits, you can drag it out of the Dock. If it's a window that's been minimized, click on it once to make it full-size, then click the red button in its top-left corner to close it.

How Much Memory (RAM) Do You Have? OS 9

OS 9: Back in Mac OS 9, to find out how much RAM you had, you went to the Apple menu and selected About This Computer. When the screen pictured above opened, the amount of RAM you had installed was displayed as Built-in Memory.

How Much Memory (RAM) Do You Have? OS X

Clicking on the More Info button launches the Apple System Profiler, which gives you a bunch (a technical term meaning lots) more detail about your Mac's memory, drives, software, favorite movie, etc.

OS X: Now, in Mac OS X, you go under the Apple menu and choose About This Mac. A dialog appears that displays the amount of installed RAM (as shown above). As you can see, the Mac shown here has 768 MB of RAM. In other words, it probably needs more RAM. How much more? A bunch. Honestly, just saying "a bunch" is kind of arbitrary. It's actually "a whole bunch." If you need more information than this, and you want to really dig under the hood and find out all the inner technical specs of your Mac (in other words, you spend a lot of time alone in your room), click on the More Info button and an application named Apple System Profiler opens; you'll be able to find out things like your Boot ROM info (mine is 4.3.7f3, just in case you were wondering). You will also be able to get useful information about your Mac.

Determining a File's Size OS 9

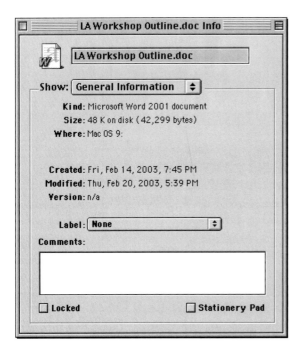

OS 9: Back in Mac OS 9, to quickly find out the size of any file, you could click on the file, then press Command-I to bring up the file's Info window, where the file size would appear, as shown above. You could also see the file's size in the Size column of the window (folder) it lived in if it was set to List view (rather than Icon view).

Determining a File's Size OS X

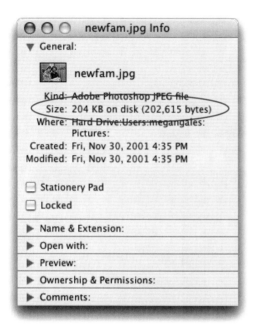

OS X: The same keyboard shortcut, Command-I (for Get Info), still applies in Mac OS X. Pressing it brings up the Get Info window (shown above) and the file size appears next to the word "Size." If you want to see the file size without bringing up the Get Info box, you can set its Finder window to either List view or Column view, and the size information is displayed.

Adding Comments to a File OS 9

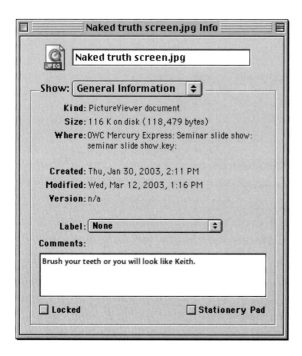

OS 9: Back in Mac OS 9, you could add your own personal comments to most any file by pressing Command-I and typing them into the Comments field at the bottom of the dialog (by comments, I mean literally anything you want to say about the file, like "This file annoys me," "I was having a bad day when I created this file," "Don't forget to delete this file after Valentine's Day," etc.). You could only view these comments in the same way—clicking on the file and pressing Command-I (Get Info).

Adding Comments to a File OS X

OS X: Now, not only can you add comments, you can actually see these comments when viewing files in a Finder window set to List view. First, add your own comments by pressing Command-I to bring up the Info window; click on the disclosure triangle before the word "Comments"; and type your comments in the white box. To view these comments, open the folder that contains your file, click the View as List button, and press Command-J to bring up the View preferences for this window. Under Show Columns, turn on the checkbox for Comments, and they'll now be visible in your window (as shown above).

Keeping a File from Being Deleted OS 9

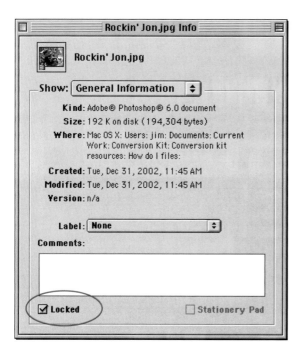

OS 9: Back in Mac OS 9, if you had a file you wanted to make sure didn't get accidentally deleted (trashed) from your hard drive, you could lock it by clicking on the file,
then pressing Command-I to bring up the Get Info window. If you checked the box
next to Locked, the file could be put in the Trash, but it wouldn't be deleted when you
emptied the Trash.

Keeping a File from Being Deleted OS X

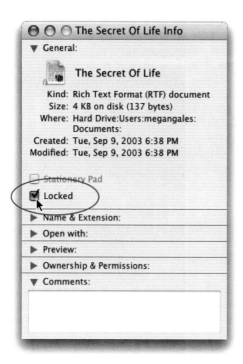

OS X: You still lock a file pretty much the same way, but the protection is better in Mac OS X. Press Command-I to bring up the Info window, and then click the Locked checkbox (as shown above). In OS 9, you could drag a locked file to the Trash, but the Trash wouldn't empty (you'd get a warning that something was locked, but it wouldn't tell you which file). But in OS X, you can't even drag a locked file into the Trash in the first place. If you try, you get the "Oh no you don't" warning dialog.

new stuff:	Another new locking feature in OS X is that you now get a visible cue to tell you a file is locked. When you lock a file, it adds a tiny padlock to the left of its icon (as shown at right) so you no longer have to press Command-I just to see if a file's locked—you can just look at the icon. Nice.	

Getting Stuff Out of the Trash OS 9

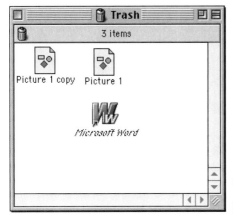

OS 9: Back in Mac OS 9, if you tossed something into the Trash and then decided you didn't want it in there after all, you could just double-click on the Trash icon on your desktop. This would open the Trash window, and you could drag your file right out.

Getting Stuff Out of the Trash OS X

OS X: Now, you can access the Trash window by going to the Dock and clicking once on the Trash icon. Drag the file you want to keep right out of the Trash window, just like in Mac OS 9. However, there's a great new feature that should keep you from digging in the Trash too often. If you drag a file to the Trash and then immediately decide you want to keep it, you have an undo. That's right, just press Command-Z to undo the trashing of that file, and it jumps right back where it came from. Now, you only get one undo, so don't trash the file, then go off and do 15 other things, and hope to undo that file back out of the Trash. At that point, you'd have to do it the old-fashioned way—click on the Trash icon and go dumpster diving.

Changing a File's Icon OS 9

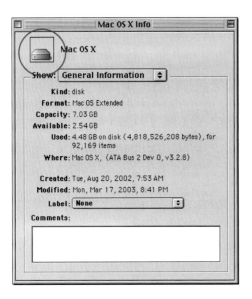

OS 9: In Mac OS 9, to copy an icon from one file to another, you'd start by clicking on the file whose icon you wanted to copy, and then press Command-I to bring up the Get Info window. Then, you'd click on the tiny icon that appears at the top left, press Command-C to copy it, then you'd close the Get Info window. Next, you would click on the file you wanted to have that icon, press Command-I to open its Info window, click on the icon at the top left of the window, and press Command-V to paste the icon you copied. Done. New icon.

Changing a File's Icon OS X

OS X: In Mac OS X, the process is the same—your basic copy and paste. Click on the file whose icon you want to steal and press Command-I. Go to the top-left corner of the Get Info box, click on the icon, and press Command-C to copy it. Now, find the file whose icon you want to change, press Command-I, click on the icon in the top-left corner, and press Command-V (the shortcut for paste, which really makes very little sense, but life is like that sometimes).

new stuff:	Here's a sweet trick: Click once on the file whose icon you want to steal. Now, press Option-Command-I to bring up its Get Info window, select its icon, and press Command-C to copy it. Then, click on any other file, and instead of having to open a new Get Info box, the file's info appears in the Info window that's already open, and its icon is already highlighted. Press Command-V to paste the new icon. While the Info window is still open, you can click on as many files as you like to change their icons as well.

Switching Applications OS 9

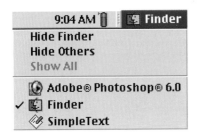

OS 9: Back in Mac OS 9, if you had more than one application open, you could switch from one to another by going to the Application Switcher at the top right-hand corner of your menu bar, where the current application's name or icon was shown. You'd click on that name and a pop-down menu would appear (the infamous Application Switcher), and you'd switch to another open app by clicking on it in that list.

Switching Applications OS X

Command-Tab steps forward through open applications. Shift-Command-Tab reverses direction.

OS X: Now in Mac OS X, you switch to another open application by simply clicking on its icon in the Dock. If you're too lazy to move your cursor all the way to the bottom of your screen, you can step through your open applications (including the Finder) by pressing Command-Tab while in your current application. A sexy-looking window with beautiful, big icons opens on top of whatever application you're currently using. Each time you press Tab, the next icon highlights (Shift-Command-Tab reverses direction). When the icon for the application you want to use is highlighted, release the Command and Tab keys and the new app becomes active.

Accessing an Application's Preferences OS 9

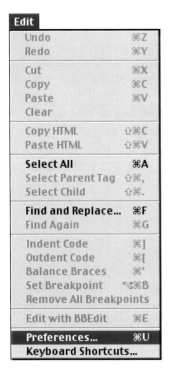

OS 9: Back in Mac OS 9, you could access most applications' customizable preferences from the application's Edit menu. Now you might think, "Isn't it odd that software developers all over the world had the exact same idea about where preferences should go?" That would be odd—freaky even. But before you start calling talk-radio shows to share your theory of a "One World Developer Alliance Conspiracy," let me present another possible explanation—Apple asked developers to put the preference settings there so it would be consistent among programs. But you can still call your radio program, because while the developers made it appear as if the preferences were in the Edit menu, they really weren't. The actual preference files were really in a folder buried in the System Folder. The name of this secret folder? "Preferences." Hang up the phone—not much of a conspiracy here. But what if they only want to make us think the preferences are in the Preferences folder? Hmmmmmm. Hand me the phone, Earl.

Accessing an Application's Preferences OS X

OS X: Now, Apple has asked software developers to place Preferences under the Application menu (which is actually the name of the application itself, to the immediate right of the Apple menu at the top-left corner of the screen). In the example shown above, the open application is Adobe Photoshop. When you select Preferences, you're actually opening a file that is in the Application Support folder which is, in turn, in the System Library. Confused? That's exactly what they want.

Putting Your Mac to Sleep OS 9

OS 9: In Mac OS 9, you had two easy ways to put your computer to sleep. The first was to go to the menu bar, select Special, and choose Sleep from the drop-down menu. The second way was to click on the Control Strip, find the Energy Saver icon (the little crescent moon on a blue star field), and choose Sleep Now.

Putting Your Mac to Sleep OS X

OS X: It's still easy in Mac OS X. Now, you click on the Apple menu and choose Sleep (as shown above).

new stuff: *On some Macs, you can press Control-Eject to bring up a dialog asking if you want to Restart, Shut Down, or Sleep.*

Keeping Your Mac from Going to Sleep OS 9

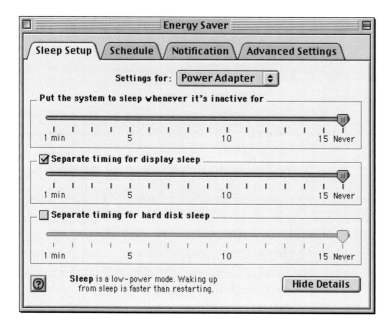

OS 9: Back in Mac OS 9, if you wanted to prevent your Mac from going to sleep on you (which was mostly a concern of PowerBook and iBook users), you poured three double-shot espressos on the keyboard. No wait—that's what happened when you tried to stay awake to get your taxes done. To keep your Mac awake, you went to the Apple menu, selected Control Panels, and chose Energy Saver. When the Energy Saver Control Panel appeared, you clicked on the Show Details button in the lower-right corner. When the dialog opened, all you had to do was move the appropriate sliders to Never.

Keeping Your Mac from Going to Sleep OS X

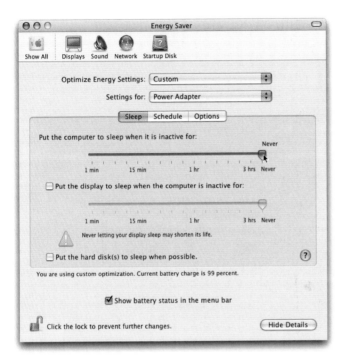

OS X: Now you set your Mac's nap time in the Energy Saver Preference pane. Go under the Apple menu, choose System Preferences, then click the Energy Saver icon. When the Energy Saver Preference pane appears, click on the Sleep button (if it's not visible, click the Details button) and move the top slider to the far right, to Never. That's it—no more sleepy bear syndrome.

new stuff:	If you're using a PowerBook or iBook, Mac OS X has some Energy Saver presets already configured based on how you're using the PowerBook or iBook. Click on the pop-up menu next to Optimize Energy Settings and select one of the options.	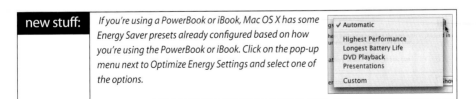

Shutting Down Your Mac OS 9

OS 9: Back in Mac OS 9, to shut down (when you were totally done working on your Mac for the day), you'd go under the Special menu and choose Shut Down.

Shutting Down Your Mac OS X

When you choose Shut Down, by default, it brings up a dialog asking, "Are you sure you want to shut down your computer now?" In Panther, if you don't make a choice in 120 seconds, it automatically shuts down for you. You can stop this somewhat annoying dialog from appearing at all by holding down the Option key before you choose Shut Down from the Apple menu.

OS X: Now, you shut down by going under the Apple menu and choosing Shut Down. On some Macs, you can shut down by pressing-and-holding the Power button. On newer Macs, pressing and releasing the power button instantly puts your Mac to sleep, or you can press Control-Eject to bring up a dialog where you can choose to Sleep, Restart, or Shut Down.

new stuff: *One of the things about OS X that takes some getting used to for some people is the fact that you really don't need to shut down your Mac unless you can't stand the thought of the pennies of electricity it's consuming on a monthly basis. When you're done for the day, let it run. Geeks routinely check Apple System Profiler to see how long their Mac has been running since the last restart. Since it's such a stable operating system, it's possible to go several weeks before you have to restart. Uptime, baby. It's all about uptime.*

Changing the Startup Disk OS 9

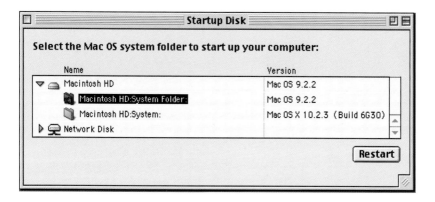

OS 9: Back "in the day," if you wanted to start up from a different drive than your current startup disk or if you wanted to start up from a different version of the operating system, you would go under the Apple menu, under Control Panels, and choose Startup Disk. The Startup Disk Control Panel would open (shown above) and you could choose to start up from any disk that had a Mac OS properly installed on it. This would often actually work.

Changing the Startup Disk OS X

OS X: Now, you choose your startup system (or disk) by going under the Apple menu and launching System Preferences. Then, click on the Startup Disk icon. The Startup Disk Preference pane appears, showing all available and valid s ystem folders. Choose one and click the Restart button. Earlier Macs could boot from either OS 9 or OS X; recent Macs boot only in Mac OS X.

Chapter Nine

 I've got to figure that, if you're reading this chapter, it's not because everything is working perfectly. You're probably here because there's a problem. Perhaps it's a dead-end job, an unfulfilling

Troubleshooting
IT'S NOT A GOOD SIGN IF YOU'RE READING THIS

marriage, or maybe it's a drinking problem. That's what it was for me. Drinking. Heavy drinking, brought on shortly after installing Mac OS X when I went looking for the familiar ambulance icon of Disk First Aid. I went straight to the Utilities folder (the warm fuzzy location it had been nearly all of my adult life), but it just wasn't there. I searched everywhere on my drive, but to no avail. I freaked. At that time, there was no book like this to tell me what happened to the little ambulance icon, so I turned to the bottle. It wasn't pretty. I remember feeling so detached, so disconnected from my previous OS experience that I let drinking get the best of me. The next morning, I woke up to find myself lying half naked on the floor of a Mexican jail, with a Windows XP installer disk in one hand and a map to Liza's house in the other. Needless to say, this was a serious wake-up call. Anyway, this chapter is probably not what it seems, because it's not about how to troubleshoot Mac OS X—every Mac book covers that—instead, in keeping with the format of this book (how to do the same things you did in OS 9, but now in OS X), it's about where Apple secretly moved all the troubleshooting stuff you're already used to using, in a lightly veiled effort to get you to fall off the wagon.

Force Quitting an Application OS 9

 Force "PictureViewer" to quit?
Clicking Force Quit causes you to lose any
unsaved changes. To avoid further problems,
restart your computer after you click Force
Quit.

(Force Quit)   **Cancel**

OS 9: Back in OS 9, if an application froze up, you could Force Quit it—which if you were lucky, would give you enough time to go to any other applications and save their open documents before you restarted (which you just about absolutely had to do, because after an application crash, you could be pretty sure that a system crash was on its way). To Force Quit an application, you'd press Command-Option-Esc. This would actually work about 50–60% of the time.

Force Quitting an Application OS X

OS X: Now, if an application freezes—no sweat, you can Force Quit it and then relaunch it and get right back to work—it doesn't take down the computer (like a Force Quit in OS 9 normally did). To Force Quit an open application, go under the Apple menu and choose Force Quit (or press the keyboard shortcut Command-Option-Esc). This brings up the Force Quit Applications dialog (shown above), and you can just click on the application you want to Force Quit, then click the Force Quit button.

new stuff:	You can also Force Quit an application by holding the Option key, then clicking on the application's icon in the Dock. A pop-up menu appears (as shown here), and you can choose Force Quit from here.	

Using Disk First Aid OS 9

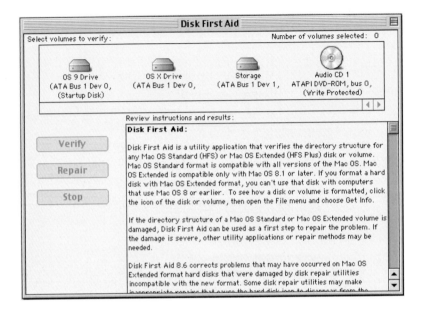

OS 9: Back in OS 9, when your Mac started acting funky, you'd run Disk First Aid. This handy little utility could repair a host of little problems that could turn into big problems. It was found in your Mac OS 9 Utilities folder, and its icon was a boxy-looking ambulance.

Using Disk First Aid OS X

OS X: Now, Disk First Aid is part of a utility called Disk Utility, which you find in the Utilities folder inside your Applications folder. When you launch Disk Utility, click on the drive you want to repair in the column on the left side of the dialog, click on the First Aid button, and then click the Repair Disk button. You can use First Aid to repair external drives, partitioned drives, etc., but not your startup drive (at least, not without going this next step). If you want to verify or repair your startup disk, you have to boot from your Mac OS X install CD. With the install CD in your drive, choose Restart from the Apple menu, then hold down the C key to force your Mac to boot from the CD rather than the hard drive. Once the startup process begins, you can release the C key. When the installer window appears, go to the menu bar at the top of the screen, click on Installer, and select Open Disk Utility to open the Disk Utility. (Did I really need to explain that part?) Now, you'll be able to choose your startup drive for verification or repair.

Force Quitting the Finder OS 9

 Force "Finder" to quit?
Clicking Force Quit causes you to lose any
unsaved changes. To avoid further problems,
restart your computer after you click Force
Quit.

(Force Quit) **Cancel**

OS 9: Back in Mac OS 9, you could Force Quit the Finder (rather than an application) by going to the Finder and pressing Option-Command-Esc. A warning dialog would appear asking, "Are you sure you want to quit the Finder?" You had a 50/50 chance of it force quitting and not bringing down your Mac (which is probably a higher percentage than you'd get when force quitting an application).

Force Quitting the Finder OS X

OS X: Now, in Mac OS X, if your Finder should get stuck, probably the fastest way to get it unstuck is to press Option-Command-Esc to bring up the Force Quit Applications dialog (shown above). Click on Finder, then press the Relaunch button. Relaunch is probably a better term than Force Quit because it doesn't really quit the Finder; instead, it relaunches the Finder (basically starts it up again). You may have to relaunch it several times before it works. Don't ask why—it's just the way it is.

Booting from Your System CD OS 9

OS 9: When all else failed in Mac OS 9, you could always boot up your Mac from the System 9 Install CD. You inserted the CD into the drive, went to the Special menu, selected Restart, then held down the C key to force the computer to boot from the CD instead of the hard drive. When the startup process was done, you could access all your drives and files. The only visible difference was that the CD showed up on the desktop as the startup drive and your desktop background was funky.

Booting from Your System CD OS X

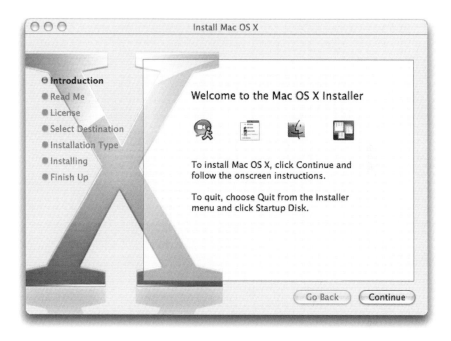

OS X: In Mac OS X, you can also boot your Mac from the system CD. Actually, that's not entirely true. Well, it could be true. It depends on what you mean by true. You can boot your Mac from the Mac OS X Install CD but, unlike Mac OS 9, you can't access your drives and data files once it's booted up. What you *can* do is run First Aid and hope it can fix your problem so you can boot from your hard drive. To run First Aid, insert the Install CD into your drive, choose Restart from the Apple Menu, then hold down the letter C to force your Mac to boot from the CD rather than the hard drive. Once the Installer window opens, go to the menu bar at the top of the screen, click on Installer, and select Open Disk Utility. Select your drive from the list on the left, click on the First Aid button, and then click on the Repair Disk button and hope for the best.

Rebuilding the Desktop OS 9

OS 9: Back in Mac OS 9, when things started to get funky with your Mac, one of the first things you'd do was rebuild the desktop. In fact, if you called Apple Tech Support, usually the first thing they'd ask you was, "Did you rebuild the desktop?" (followed by, "Did you zap the PRAM?" followed by, "Are you sure you actually own an Apple computer?"). To rebuild the desktop in Mac OS 9, you'd choose Restart from the Special menu, then as your Mac was restarting, just before the desktop appeared, you'd hold down the Option and Command keys. This would bring up a dialog asking, "Are you sure you want to Rebuild the Desktop on Scott's Mac?" (I always thought this was pretty weird for people who weren't named Scott.) If you clicked OK, a status dialog would appear showing a sloth-like progress bar (it was actually more like a "no progress" bar) until the desktop was rebuilt.

Rebuilding the (Classic) Desktop OS X

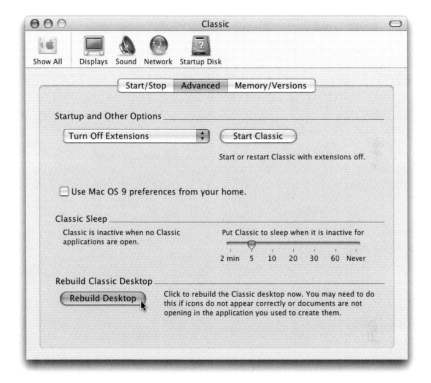

OS X: Now, although there's no need to rebuild the desktop for Mac OS X, if you run any Classic environment applications (apps that haven't been updated to run under Mac OS X) you'll still need to rebuild the desktop for the Classic environment when problems arise. Luckily, it's easier to rebuild the Classic environment desktop than it was in Mac OS 9. Now, you simply go under the Apple menu, choose System Preferences, and in the resulting dialog, click on the Classic icon. When the Classic preferences appear, click on the Advanced button, then under Rebuild Classic Desktop, click on the Rebuild Desktop button. That's all there is to it.

Erasing and Reformatting a Drive OS 9

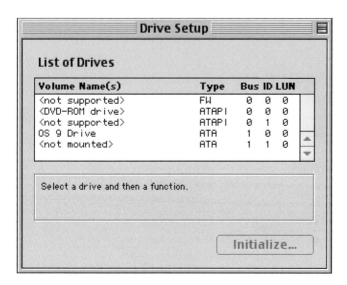

OS 9: To erase and format a drive in Mac OS 9, you opened the utility called Drive Setup, selected the drive you wanted to erase from a list of attached drives, chose a format, gave it a name, and clicked Erase.

Erasing and Reformatting a Drive OS X

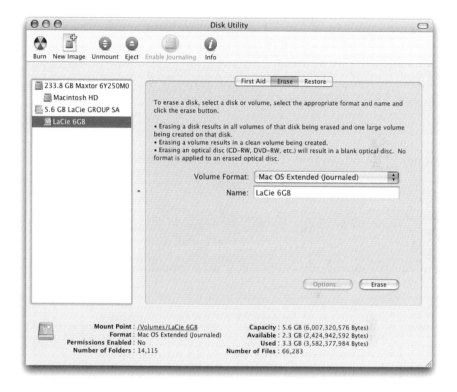

OS X: Erasing a drive is pretty much the same in Mac OS X, except the utility you use is now called, imaginatively, Disk Utility. You can find it in the Utilities folder inside the Applications folder. When you launch Disk Utility, click on the Erase button. Locate the drive you want to erase (it can be any drive except the one that's currently running Mac OS X) and click on it. Now, look at the drive you've highlighted and make sure it's really the one you want to erase because if you erase the wrong one, you're going to have a very bad day. Select the Volume Format from the pop-up menu, type in the name you want the drive to have, check one more time that you've selected the right drive (I'm not paranoid—really—just experienced), and click the Erase button. You get a warning to let you know this is serious stuff and to make sure you know what you're about to do. Click Erase and you're done.

Using Simple Finder OS 9

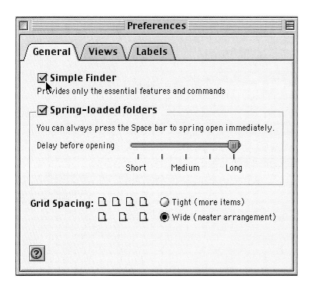

OS 9: In Mac OS 9, to turn on Simple Finder, you would go under the File menu, to Finder Preferences, then turn on Simple Finder.

Using Simple Finder OS X

OS X: Now, to set your Mac to display just the Simple Finder, go under the Apple menu, choose System Preferences, then click on the Accounts icon. When the Accounts Preference pane appears, click on the account you want to restrict, then click on the Limitations button and choose the degree of limitations you want to put in place for this user (including the Simple Finder). Don't see a Limitations button? That's because you're a positive thinker. The word is simply not in your vocabulary. You scoff at limits. You laugh at limits. Limits are for losers. Whatever. Actually, if there's not a Limitations button, it's because the owner of the account has administrative privileges on the Mac. You can't limit an administrator. They're positive thinkers. They scoff at limits. They...

Restarting Your Mac OS 9

OS 9: In Mac OS 9, Macs actually crashed. (I know, that's hard to believe, but it did happen from time to time. Okay, it happened daily. Well, not daily, but at least weekly. Well, not for everybody, but for some people. Mean people mostly.) If things started acting wonky, or if one of your applications crashed (which basically meant you better restart soon before all hell breaks loose), you would restart by going under the Special menu and choosing Restart. You could also use the keyboard shortcut Control-Command-Delete (which was especially helpful if your screen was frozen and, therefore, you couldn't get to the Special menu).

Restarting Your Mac OS X

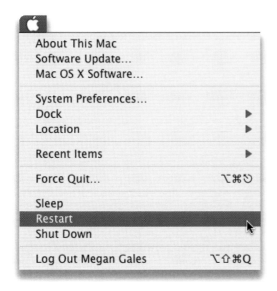

OS X: Now, you don't need to restart because OS X never, ever crashes. Okay, that's a bit of an exaggeration; actually, now the system very rarely crashes. (I know some people using Mac OS X that have yet to have a system crash. I call these people "liars." Kidding.) Should you need to restart, you now find it under the Apple menu (as shown above). You can also press Control-Eject on newer machines to bring up a dialog where you can choose to Sleep, Shut Down, or Restart.

Using Apple's Built-In Help OS 9

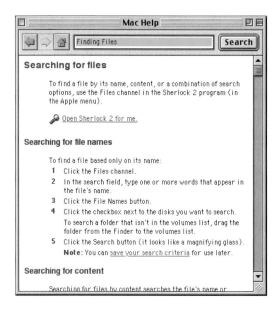

OS 9: Back in Mac OS 9, you could access Apple's built-in Help function (called the Apple Help Viewer) by choosing Help from the Help menu.

Using Apple's Built-In Help OS X

OS X: In Mac OS X, just choose Mac Help from the Help menu, or press Command-?. This brings up the new-and-improved Help Viewer (shown above). You can phrase questions like "What's the capital of Vermont?" or, if you actually want a chance of getting an answer, enter something more along the lines of "How do I delete a file?" or "Where is the Trash can?." When you click on one of the myriad answers that it returns (sorted by possible relevance by default), a brief synopsis of the answer appears at the bottom left of the screen. If that sounds like the answer you're looking for, double-click on it and a more complete answer appears.

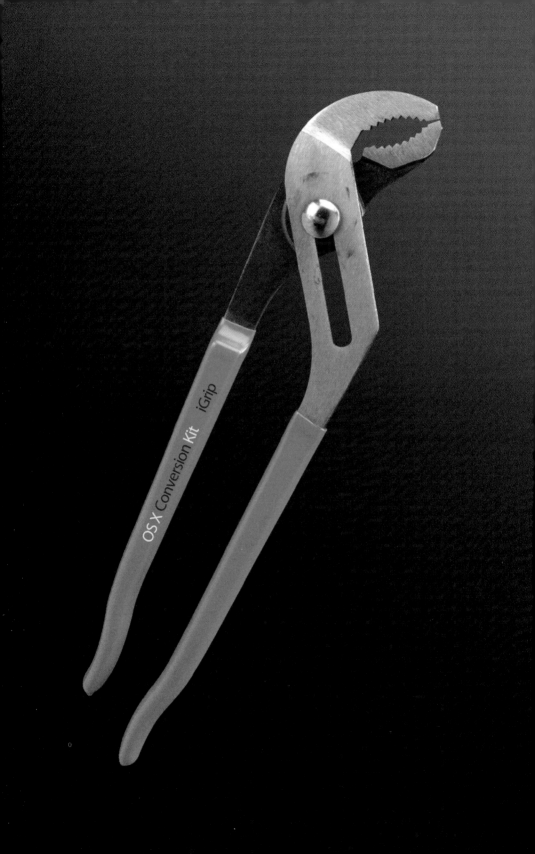

Chapter Ten

X If you've bought a Mac in the last year or so, it came with Mac OS X pre-installed, so you skipped the whole terrifying Mac OS X installation procedure. Now, is installing Mac OS X really that scary? Not if you have the

Don't Freak Out
INSTALLING MAC OS X, AND OTHER SCARY STUFF

answers to the questions the Installer Assistant asks you. Here's the catch—you won't. Oh, somebody, somewhere probably has the answers (perhaps a high-ranking Apple employee or Stephen Hawking) but not people like you and me. So, what's the best course of action when faced with these questions? Guess. That's what I did, and my Mac works just fine. Actually, I'm exaggerating (a bit). In fact, the installation process is surprisingly simple if you're an Apple authorized service tech. See, I'm kidding—you fell for it again. Honestly, it's a breeze, but there are a number of questions it will ask you that might freak you out. Primarily because you have to give your answers in Portuguese, and spelling counts. Again, just a joke. Besides the things that might freak you out during installation (few though they may be), there are a number of other things that might make you spaz, so I covered those too. (By the way, the term "spaz" is actually derived from the Portuguese word "spazzulita," which loosely translated means "one who has installed Mac OS X but cannot speak Portuguese and therefore cannot answer critical installation questions.")

1. Do I Really Need All This Stuff?

If you install everything that's included on your Mac OS X Install CDs, you will likely fill more drive space than the combined capacity of the first five hard drives you owned—it's huge. Here are some of the options you'll have when you install to help you sort out what you need and what you can leave on the CD.

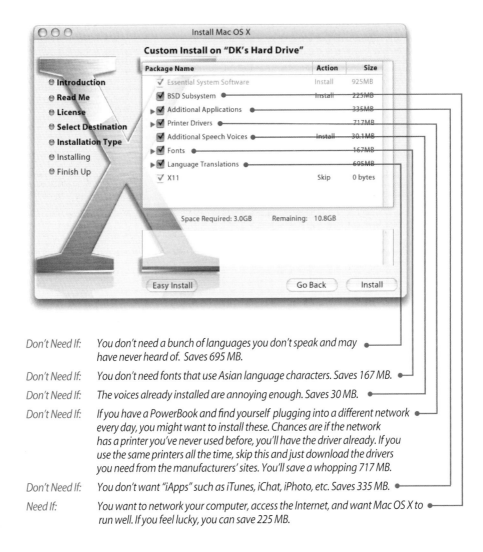

Don't Need If: You don't need a bunch of languages you don't speak and may have never heard of. Saves 695 MB.

Don't Need If: You don't need fonts that use Asian language characters. Saves 167 MB.

Don't Need If: The voices already installed are annoying enough. Saves 30 MB.

Don't Need If: If you have a PowerBook and find yourself plugging into a different network every day, you might want to install these. Chances are if the network has a printer you've never used before, you'll have the driver already. If you use the same printers all the time, skip this and just download the drivers you need from the manufacturers' sites. You'll save a whopping 717 MB.

Don't Need If: You don't want "iApps" such as iTunes, iChat, iPhoto, etc. Saves 335 MB.

Need If: You want to network your computer, access the Internet, and want Mac OS X to run well. If you feel lucky, you can save 225 MB.

2. Where's All the Stuff I Had on My Desktop?

In a recent poll of persons planning on upgrading to Mac OS X, when asked their greatest fear about the upgrade, 50% responded, "I'm afraid I'm going to lose some important stuff." (I won't tell you what the other person said—suffice it to say they need therapy.)

When you see the beautiful aqua desktop for the first time, you will not see all the folders and icons you had so neatly arranged on your desktop in Mac OS 9. Don't freak out—all your stuff is safe; it's just moved to a folder called "Desktop (Mac OS 9)." All of your old applications are still there, too, in a folder named "Applications (Mac OS 9)."

OS X: You've heard the horror stories. You've read the comments of people in the forums who were one page away from finishing their doctoral dissertation when they installed Mac OS X and started sobbing uncontrollably as they booted up their Mac and their work of the past three years wasn't on the desktop where they left it. They can deal with the dissertation—it's their extensive collection of bookmarks to Klingon and Cardassian language discussion forums that has them upset. You won't lose a thing when you upgrade to Mac OS X—files, applications, e-mails, bookmarks—they're all safe.

3. Why Is Mac OS 9 Opening?

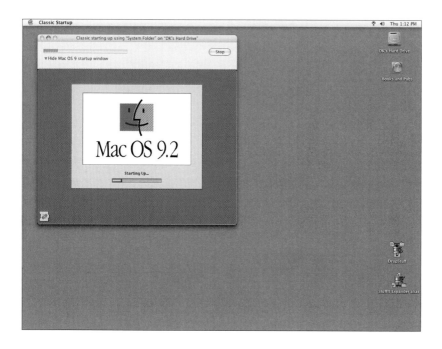

OS X: If you launch an application, and something that looks like Mac OS 9 starts opening in a new window on the desktop, don't freak out. It's just Mac OS 9 opening in a new window on the desktop. While Mac OS X is the latest, greatest operating system available on the planet, there are still some applications which haven't yet been rewritten to be able to run in it. When you open a document created with one of these applications (officially known as Classic apps, but commonly called Lame apps), Mac OS X opens the Classic environment and runs the application with Mac OS 9. There's another group of applications (known as Carbon apps) that can run in *both* Mac OS X and the Classic environment. If you have one of those applications, and want to run it in Classic (I don't know why you would, but it's certainly possible that somewhere, someone might), you can click on the application, press Command-I, then in the Info window, click on the checkbox for "Open in the Classic environment." The third group consists of applications written to take full advantage of Mac OS X's power, a.k.a. Native or Cocoa apps.

4. Sorry, Dave. I'm Afraid I Can't Let You Do That.

OS X: One thing that freaks people out in Mac OS X is the area of permission. The first time you run across it will probably be when you go to install an application, and before it will let you, it asks you to enter your administrator password so it can make sure you're actually allowed to install a program on this machine. It gets even uglier when you attempt to drag a file into or out of a folder or to the Trash and you get a warning that there is no way you are going to be allowed to move that file. There are several reasons why you get such warnings. It might be as simple as "the file is locked" to prevent accidental erasure; or it could be that whoever owns the file doesn't want you messing with it. If you're on a network, the system administrator may not have given you full privileges. So how do you get around this? If you're trying to delete something, go ask your administrator if he'll let you toss something in the Trash (and don't forget to say please). If you're trying to install something, ask the administrator either to install it or to share his password—which is pretty unlikely because then he loses his "God-like" control over your Mac.

5. You're Locked Out of a Preference

OS X: If you don't know what you're doing and engage in casual clicking, dragging, and deleting, it's possible to really mess up your Mac. Mac OS X allows anyone who is an administrator to lock certain System Preferences to keep users from messing with them, which can prevent some major headaches. Two groups of people put this feature to good use: parents and network administrators. How do you get around this? Parents—don't bother trying. Network administrators—take them out for drinks, get 'em hammered, and then ask them to give you the password. This works at least six to seven times out of ten.

6. There's More Than One Library Folder

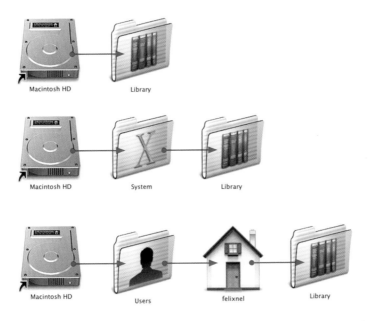

OS X: Libraries can be confusing to people moving from Mac OS 9 to Mac OS X for two reasons: First, there were none in Mac OS 9 and, second, there are at least three of them in Mac OS X. The reason for and functioning of the multiple Libraries is linked directly to Mac OS X's multiuser environment. In Mac OS 9, the "behind the scenes" functions of your Mac were handled by Control Panels, Extensions, and other items in the System Folder. In Mac OS X, the files that "run" your Mac are located in Libraries. Items needed for all users (fonts, applications, etc.) are in the main Library and can be accessed by anyone with an account. Items that can only be accessed by an administrator are kept in the Library within the System folder. Finally, every user has a Library, accessible only to them, containing files necessary for creating their desktop, preference settings, etc. So if you're looking for your browser bookmark file, for example, you would look in the Preferences folder within your user Library. If you want to add a desktop picture that can be used by anyone with an account on your Mac, you would put it in the main Library.

7. My Fonts Are Everywhere!

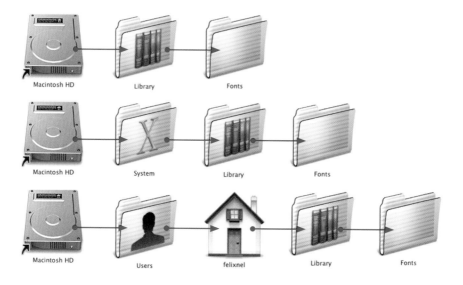

OS X: The first time you start clicking your way around your hard drive after install-ing Mac OS X, I guarantee you'll think it's déjà vu all over again because it'll seem that everywhere you turn, you're running into a Fonts folder. There are a lot of places you can store fonts in Mac OS X depending on whom you want to be able to access them. One thing you don't want to do is mess with the Fonts folder that is within the Library folder, within the System folder. You might never even have known about this folder since it's buried so deep, but now that I've told you about it, you're tempted to go and mess with it, aren't you? Don't do it. Bad things can happen. If fonts are freaking you out, go to Chapter Six for more information.

8. Disk Images and Packages

When you download an application, it usually arrives compressed. Sometimes this process (from compressed file to mounted disk) happens automatically, but sometimes you need to click an icon.

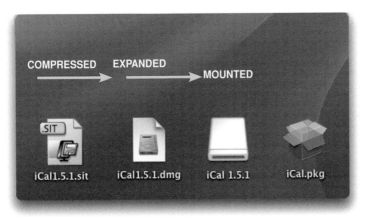

When you click on the mounted drive image on your desktop, you see the application installer, which is often a package.

OS X: Mac OS X often uses disk images as part of the installation process for an application. They can freak you out a bit the first time because, well . . . they're different. You run across them mostly when you download an application from the Web and you go to your desktop looking for the app you just downloaded and instead find three files with very similar names (you don't always see three—sometimes it's only two), including one that ends with the suffix .dmg. Mac users have had the ability to create disk images (.dmg files) with Disk Copy for some time, but Mac OS X is the first operating system to use them widely. (*Note:* Disk Copy is now a part of Disk Utilty found in the Utilities folder in the Applications folder.) Packages, on the other hand, are new to Mac OS X. They are essentially a special type of folder that holds an application and all its support files. But unlike the application folders you're accustomed to in Mac OS 9, clicking on a package doesn't open a window showing the application file along with all the supports; it simply launches the application.

9. Where's the Chooser?

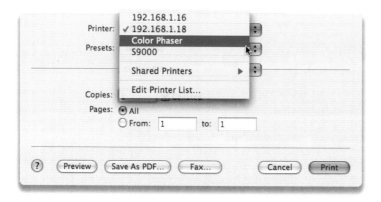

OS X: In Mac OS 9, if you wanted to select a printer or log into a network, you went to the Chooser. In Mac OS X, the Chooser is gone. Instead, you now choose your printer directly from the Print dialog of the application you're printing from, saving untold confusion. Chapter Six has more on selecting printers. Logging into networks is easier, too—now you can access a network from the menu bar of any Finder window (see Chapter Seven).

10. Optimizing System Performance

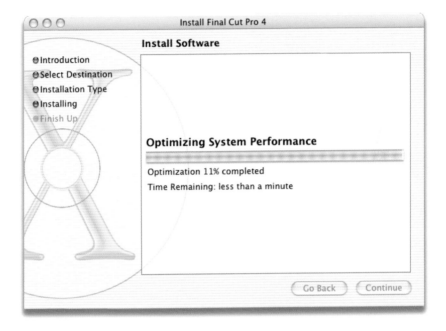

OS X: This one is guaranteed to drive you crazy. It happens after you install some applications. (If it happened every time, for all apps, then it wouldn't be confusing. The only pattern I've been able to figure out is that it usually occurs when you're in a hurry. Like when the flight attendant announces that the plane can't take off until the passenger in 19C turns off their laptop. All you were doing was installing a game to play on the flight. It's almost as if your Mac detects you're in a hurry [kind of like how dogs sense fear] because the bigger the hurry, the longer the optimization process takes.) It really does serve a vital purpose, but I won't bore you with the technical details, even though I really do know them. I just wanted to let you know about it so you won't freak out when it happens.

Chapter Eleven

9 I know what you're thinking—there are only 20 cool things? Of course not, there are loads of things you can do in Mac OS X that you couldn't do in Mac OS 9, but some of them are (a) automatic, (b) too big to be called little things

20 Cool Little Things You Couldn't Do in Mac OS 9

(like preemptive multitasking, protected memory, etc.), and (c) I can't think of a "c" right now. Some things are actually fairly major, but those features didn't make it into Apple's ads—like the new Finder Window Sidebar. It's pretty darn handy, and chances are you'll be using it every day, but it doesn't get the press like "preemptive multitask-ing" does. Why does preemptive multitasking get all the press? It's simple. Preemptive multitasking has hired its own Washington-based lobbyists and an L.A.-based PR firm to make sure it stays in the public eye. How do you think all those photos of J. Lo and Preemptive Multitasking dining at a trendy Hollywood bistro got on the cover of the *Enquirer*? You think some Hollywood reporter just happened to be dining at (insert Hollywood bistro name here), looked up, saw J. Lo and PM (that's his street name), and started snapping shots with his D-100? Not bloody likely. Those were set-ups. Mini-events concocted by the PR firms to make it look like PM is a player, that he's "out there" and making some noise. In reality, PM spends most nights alone, in front of the TV, with a cheap bottle of wine and take-out fajitas from Chili's.

1. Managing Your Fonts OS X

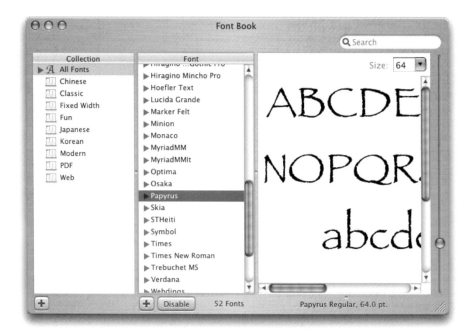

OS X: One thing the Mac never had was decent built-in font management. You could buy third-party apps that would let you manage fonts, but otherwise, you were on your own. Totally. And if there was a single part of the Mac experience that really threw people for a loop—it was fonts. In Mac OS 10.1 through 10.2, it got even more confusing. But now (in Panther), you get Font Book, and for the first time, real font management is built right in. Now you can open, close, view, and manage all of your fonts easily. Sure, it took 18 years to bring built-in font management to the Mac, but hey, who's counting? You'll find Font Book inside the Applications folder. When you launch it, by default, it shows all of your open fonts. Click on any font to see a preview of that font in the panel on the far right. To change the font size, use the vertical slider on the far right of the Preview panel. To create your own custom set of fonts (so you can open only the fonts you want), click the little plus symbol at the bottom-left corner of the Collection panel, then name your collection. To add a font to your collection, just drag it from the Font list (the center panel) to your Collection. To move multiple fonts, Command-click on each font to select it.

2. Exposé OS X

OS X: This is arguably the best thing anyone's ever done, on any platform, to reduce desktop clutter. This brilliant feature, called Exposé, is the feature that always gets spontaneous applause when I show it to a group. I'm going to attempt to explain it here, but honestly, there is absolutely no written explanation that compares with seeing it in action (even Hemingway tried, and it was his inability to adequately convey this concept that supposedly led him to drinking). First, the problem: You have multiple windows open from multiple applications, and even though you're working in one app (like Photoshop), you can see Quark's windows, several of Safari's Web browser windows, and your Finder windows all in the background. Now, you just press F9 (or move your cursor into a corner of the screen that you determine in the System Preferences), and instantly (and I mean instantly), every window shrinks down and lines up in rows across your screen so you can clearly see every single window. Move your cursor over any "shrunken" window and the window highlights and displays its name. Click on it, and that window comes to front, and all the others go back to regular size. I told you it was hard to explain, but try it once—you'll use it forever.

3. Apple Remote Desktop OS X

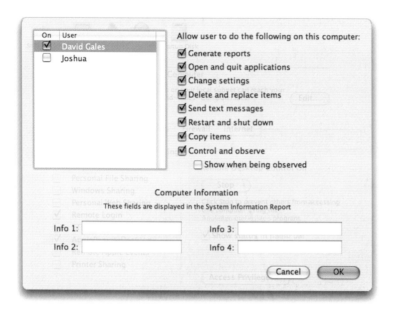

OS X: It used to be that networks were something you only had at work. Actually, once upon a time, computers were something you only had at work. Now, it's likely that you have multiple computers at home running on a small network. (I just counted—we have three laptops and two desktops at my house.) Keeping multiple machines current can be a part-time job. For several years, Apple has had a product called Apple Remote Desktop that allows one person to manage multiple computers from one location. Mac OS X includes the client software for Remote Desktop. If you purchase the Administrator software, you can observe or control any of the Macs on your network from your machine. You also can install software, configure preferences, check software versions, and run backups from wherever you happen to be. So grab a tall, cold drink, sink into your lounge chair on the pool deck, boot up your PowerBook, and survey your Mac kingdom.

4. iTunes Music Store OS X

OS X: With the release of iTunes 4 for Mac OS X, Apple introduced the coolest of the cool things—the iTunes Music Store. How cool is it? So cool that *Time Magazine* named it "Invention of the Year" in its "Coolest Inventions of 2003." When you log into the iTunes Music Store using iTunes, you have more than 400,000 songs available for download for only 99¢ each. No more lying awake nights feeling guilty for download-ing illegal MP3s. Want to make sure it's still as great a song as you remember it in the somewhat hazy days of the '60s or '70s? No problem. You can listen to a 30-second sample before you buy. A cutting-edge compression codec, Advanced Audio Coding (or AAC for those who don't want to sound like a total geek), delivers files that are smaller than MP3s, but are nearly indistinguishable from the original CD (dogs can hear a slight difference but not enough to diminish their listening experience). Load up your Mac, put 'em on your iPod, burn CDs to listen to in the car…all legally.

5. iStuff OS X

OS X: In Mac OS 9, you had a couple of "i" programs: iMovie and iTunes. Both great programs, mind you, but after the success of those two, Apple starting introducing more wonderful iStuff, exclusively for Mac OS X. These new "Digital Hub" apps include iPhoto (an absolutely amazing application for sorting, viewing, printing, and organizing your digital photos); iChat (a way-cool chat application); iCal (probably the most ingenious computer-based calendar ever); and iSync (for syncing your Mac and your iPod or handheld Palm-like device). Also, all the new-and-improved versions of iMovie and iTunes are available ONLY to OS X users. Another reason you'll be glad you switched.

6. Real Video Conferencing OS X

OS X: Before Mac OS X, video conferencing from computer to computer was pretty much a joke. The video and audio were usually out of sync, the picture looked like the original TV transmissions beamed from the lunar landing in 1969, and the audio was AM radio quality at best. But Mac OS X's iChat AV changed all that. Besides the iTunes Music Store, I don't know if there's anything Apple's done in recent history that has won as much praise from the national media as iChat's video conferencing. Besides the iChat feature (whose audio is even amazingly pristine), Apple offers a brilliantly designed "iSight" mini-camera and microphone designed to be easily mounted onto your Mac. Once you try iChat, it changes everything. This is groundbreaking stuff.

7. Controlling Music Playing in iTunes OS X

OS X: If you were playing a song with iTunes in OS 9 and you wanted to do anything—change songs, pause a song, repeat it, etc., you had to leave the program you were in, switch to iTunes, and then make your adjustments. But in OS X, you're just one click away, without leaving your current app. Control-click on the iTunes icon in the Dock and up pops a menu where you can control any songs you have playing (as shown above).

8. Deleting Files Securely OS X

Finder
About Finder
Preferences...   ⌘,
Empty Trash...   ⇧⌘⌫
Secure Empty Trash
Services   ▶
Hide Finder   ⌘H
Hide Others   ⌥⌘H
Show All

OS X: Back in OS 9, if you put a file in the Trash and then emptied the Trash, you felt it was deleted from your drive. That was a nice feeling—it just wasn't the truth. In fact, a 13-year-old kid with reasonable Macintosh experience could recover your trashed file in less than 30 seconds. Not so in Panther, because you can now also choose "Secure Empty Trash," which trashes the living daylights out of a file. In fact, it deletes your files so securely that even teen whiz kids who work for the CIA won't be able to recover them—they're gone forever—so don't choose Secure Empty Trash unless you really, really want what's in your trash gone forever and ever, amen.

new stuff:	*Mac OS X takes security to a whole new level with FileVault. This is an on-the-fly encryption algorithm that password-protects your entire Home directory. If you don't have the password, you flat don't get in, and you can kiss the entire contents of your Home directory goodbye (not even Apple can help if you forget your password). You'll find FileVault under the Apple menu, under System Preferences. This is serious mojo—use it with care.*

9. Sidebar OS X

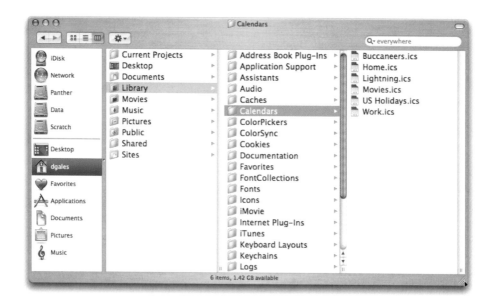

OS X: The first thing you probably noticed when you started up your Mac with Panther was the bar at the left side of all your Finder windows that has icons for some of the things you'll probably be using frequently. After extensive focus-group tests, Apple came up with a clever name for this bar at the the the side of the window: the "Sidebar." Geez, they're so creative. No matter which window view you choose (Icon, List, or Column), the Sidebar is always visible. The top portion of the Sidebar shows your hard disks, mounted drives, removable media, etc. The bottom portion allows you to drop in (or remove) folders, documents, applications, or whatever else you want to put there, making them all only one click away. Yeah, it sounds a lot like the Dock (because it is a lot like the Dock). Where it beats the Dock is in getting at the contents of a folder because you're already in a Finder window.

10. Force Quitting Without Crashing OS X

OS X: Every once in a while, Mac OS 9 would let you try to Force Quit a frozen application. It only allowed this once in a while, because it was usually so busy trying to crash your entire Mac, it really didn't care about anything else. It was usually pretty successful in crashing or freezing your whole system; so getting the opportunity to actually Force Quit in Mac OS 9 was a cause of great celebration, because you might— just might—have enough time to save open documents in other applications. Luckily, in Mac OS X, if an application freezes (hey, it happens once in a while), you can safely Force Quit (using the dialog shown above) and go on about your business. You can relaunch the frozen app or go and do something else—it doesn't matter, it doesn't "bring down" your Mac. To Force Quit a running application, just go under the Apple menu and choose Force Quit to bring up the dialog shown above, click on the name of the application you want to quit, then press the Force Quit button.

11. Faxing or Making a PDF from Any App OS X

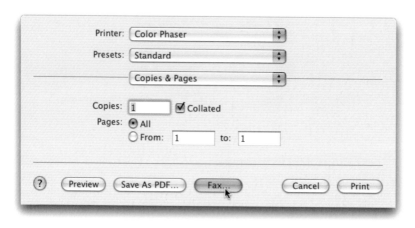

OS X: In Mac OS 9, if you wanted to fax a document, you basically had to buy a third-party application, but in Mac OS X, you can fax any document directly from the application's print dialog (you'll see a little button called Fax). Click that button, and all you have to do is enter the number where you want the document faxed, enter your cover page info, and hit Fax. Pretty darn sweet. If you want to create a PDF of your document, which anyone with Adobe Reader (previously called Acrobat Reader and available free from Adobe) can view regardless of computer platform, click the Save As PDF button in the lower left of the dialog. Give the file a name and a destination, and you're done.

12. Locking Access to Preferences OS X

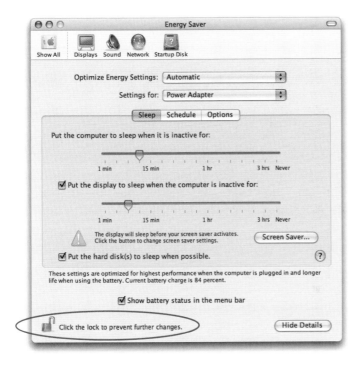

OS X: If you have particular System Preferences set just the way you like them and you don't want some goober messing around with them, you can lock these preferences to prevent further changes by clicking on the Lock icon in the bottom left-hand corner of key System Preference panes (as shown above). This means, of course, that if you later decide to make changes, you need to use your Admin User password to unlock the preferences.

13. Resizing Icons in Icon View OS X

OS X: You didn't have much control over the size of icons when you viewed a window in Icon view back in Mac OS 9. But if you want big icons in Mac OS X, you got 'em. Just open a Finder window in Icon view, press Command-J to bring up the View Options (as shown above), then drag the Icon Size slider to the right to make them larger and to the left to make them smaller. You can also choose to have this apply to all windows or just to this one by selecting one of the options at the top of the dialog.

14. Previewing Movies/Audio in Column View OS X

OS X: Now if you have a QuickTime video clip, or an audio file, you can get a live pre-view of the contents of that file, as long as you're in Column view (as shown above). Just click on the movie or audio clip, and the QuickTime window appears, enabling you to preview the clip right within the Finder window, rather than having to launch the QuickTime player.

15. Taking Advantage of UNIX OS X

OS X: By now, you've probably heard that Mac OS X is based on the UNIX platform, and you probably know that's a good thing (even if you don't know why). But besides the stability and power of UNIX, one of the coolest things about it is that you can use it to "hack" (a geek-chic word for "customize") your system. It's amazing the level of customization you can achieve by simply typing a few command lines of UNIX code in Mac OS X's Terminal application (found in the Application folder, within the Utilities folder). In fact, there are entire books written on UNIX commands you can use to customize your Mac. A great place online to find some great UNIX hacks for Mac OS X is www.macosxhints.com (in the sidebar on the right side of their site, where it says "Hints by Topics," choose UNIX from the pop-up list, then press "Go"). You'll find some very cool stuff there indeed. Just a word of advice: You'll notice that most tips start with "Remember to back up your hard drive first." That's because when you're hacking your system, "You're hacking your system!" and if you mess up, it can really mess things up. In short: UNIX isn't for wusses.

16. Naming with More than 31 Characters OS X

Really, you can name this file pretty much anything you want, and the name field will just keep expanding. Not bad, eh?

OS X: The maximum file name length of 31 characters has been lifted, and you've got the okay to start going crazy by naming files with up to 256 characters. Just click on a file, start typing, and long names automatically wrap to the next line. *Warning*: This is a dangerous tip because if you do not use restraint, you're going to make people very angry if you start e-mailing them files that have entire paragraphs for file names. Like many things in life—just because you can doesn't mean you necessarily should.

17. Seeing Folder/File Info in Icon View OS X

OS X: Now, if you want to know how many items are in a folder, you can turn on Show Item Info (by opening a window, pressing Command-J, and turning on Show Item Info as shown above), and when viewed in Icon view, the number of items in a folder appears just below each folder (as shown above). Another cool thing is that QuickTime movie icons, when viewed in this fashion, display their running length.

18. Viewing Windows in Column View OS X

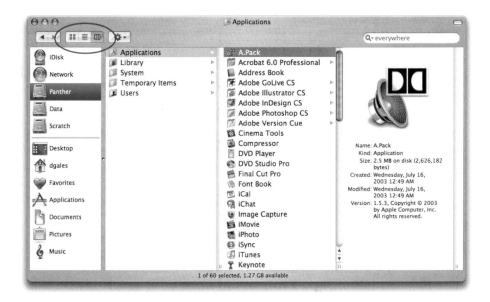

OS X: There's a new way to view and navigate your Finder windows in Mac OS X, and that's Column view (shown above). This lets you quickly scroll to the right, expanding folders as you go, to get to your desired files, rather than having to open folder after folder. I know people who love this new Column view with every fiber of their being, and although I agree it's a wonderful new addition to Mac OS X, I still can't help but worry about these people, at least on some level.

19. Seeing Thumbnail Previews of Icons OS X

OS X: In Mac OS 9, if your photos didn't have thumbnail-icon previews, you saw generic icons instead (and incidentally, most digital-camera photos use the generic JPEG icon). But in Icon view of Mac OS X, if you turn on Show Icon Preview, it automatically replaces these generic icons with full-color previews of the images (as shown above). To turn this feature on, open a window, press Command-J to open the View Options, then turn on the Show Icon Preview checkbox.

20. Adding Menu Bar Controls OS X

OS X: The Control Strip from Mac OS 9 is a thing of the past. It's been replaced with something much less intrusive, and much more convenient—menu bar items. The checkboxes to turn on individual menu bar items are found in the System Preferences for specific features (e.g., to turn on the Sound menu bar item, go to the Sound System Preferences). Now, you can access things like your system volume, monitor resolution, AirPort, and modem controls directly from the top-right side of your menu bar. Just click on the menu item and a drop-down menu appears (as shown).

Chapter Twelve

Are there really things you could do back in Mac OS 9 that you can't do using today's new-and-improved Mac OS X? Sadly, yes. Not many, mind you, but a few. These are the things we don't talk about at Mac parties (okay, they're not

20 Little Things Apple Changed Just to Mess with Your Head

ACTUALLY, THERE'S A METHOD BEHIND THEIR MADNESS. AT LEAST THAT'S WHAT WE'VE BEEN LED TO BELIEVE.

really parties, they're more like loosely organized self-help meetings with group-therapy overtones). But more than looking at how your #1 all-time favorite feature from Mac OS 9 didn't make the trip over to Mac OS X, this chapter looks at things you don't need to do anymore. You see, there were things— horrible, unspeakable things—that you used to have to do that you just don't have to anymore. One thing that's gone is the constant praying. Mac OS 9 users spent a part of each day silently praying that the application they were running wouldn't freeze, because they knew that if it did, it would bring down their entire machine. There are lots of good reasons to pray (Lotto being one), but wasting good quality prayers on having your Mac OS not crash was counterproductive (especially since God has His hands full with prayer requests from Windows users, which apparently start before the average Windows user even boots their machine, and continues for hours after they've shut down). So this chapter is really lots of good news, sprinkled with tiny particles of bad news (namely numbers 2, 3, 8, 11, 12, and 17. Okay, maybe 18 and 20, too).

1. Put Away Is Gone, Undo Is Here

OS X: In Mac OS 9, if you moved a file out of a folder, you could usually click on that file, press Command-Y (the shortcut for the Put Away command), and that file would jump back to its original folder. This was particularly helpful when you dragged something into the Trash, and then changed your mind—Command-Y would put the selected file back where it came from. In Mac OS X, this command has been replaced and expanded by Undo. Whereas Put Away just put stuff away, Undo reverses most Finder functions. For example, if you carefully sort through a folder of digital photos, selecting the ones you want to move to a new folder, then drag them to the wrong folder, press Command-Z and they all go back into the original folder (still selected), where you can grab them again and put them in the right folder. Or if you highlight an icon, change the name, then change your mind, Undo changes it back. (Put Away would be of no help.)

2. No Window Shade: Minimize Instead

OS X: Mac OS 9's Window Shade feature (the ability to double-click on the title bar of an open Finder window and have it roll up like a window shade, leaving just the title bar still visible) is gone. In Mac OS X, when you double-click an open window, instead of "rolling up," it minimizes to the Dock. In some ways, this is better than the old Window Shade feature because it removes the window from the desktop area altogether, making things less cluttered than in Mac OS 9.

3. Scrapbook Is Long Gone

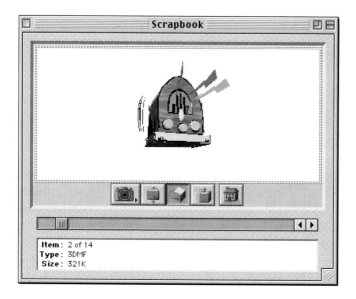

OS X: In Mac OS 9, you could copy and paste low-resolution graphics into a Scrapbook Utility. Then, if you needed to use one of these low-res graphics, you could open the Scrapbook, scroll to the desired graphic, copy it, and paste it into an open application. Since the Scrapbook only supported low-resolution graphics, it was of little use, so in Mac OS X, it's gone, and it really hasn't been replaced by anything. In short, "She's gone-on-on-on-on-on, oh-oh-oh-I-I, I better learn to how to face it...."

4. There's No Trash Can on the Desktop

OS X: The famous Macintosh Trash can no longer lives on the desktop (as it did in all previous versions of the Mac OS); it's now located at the far right of the Dock. What if you don't want it at the far right of the Dock? Tough. That's where they put it and that's where it stays. Try to move it—go ahead. Just can't play by the rules, can you? Always have to push the envelope (that's why you're a Mac user).

5. The Special Menu Is Gone

OS X: The Special menu in Mac OS 9 held a number of commands, like Shut Down, Erase, Eject, and Restart. The Special menu is gone in Mac OS X and these commands have, for the most part, moved under the Apple menu. See Chapter Eight for how to shut down, eject a disk, erase a file, and restart you computer.

6. SimpleText Is Now TextEdit

OS X: Remember SimpleText? It was a great little program. It launched faster than a greased pig, and although it lacked a few key things (like a spell checker), it was pretty handy for a quick note. Well, in Mac OS X, it's been replaced by TextEdit, which still launches as fast as an oily squealer (with no splash screen to slow things down). TextEdit is Mac OS X-native, which means that it offers features such as Services, font preview, and special characters not available before. It also has lots of word processor-like features, such as enhanced control of fonts, type tweaking, the ability to create custom styles, and spell checking. One thing I really love about TextEdit is that it opens Microsoft Word documents and saves documents as Word documents.

7. Virtual Memory Is Virtually Gone

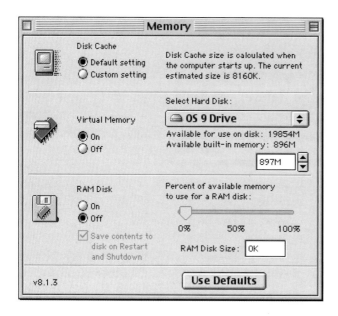

OS X: Back in Mac OS 9, you could set aside a chunk of your empty hard drive space to be used as Virtual Memory—a slower form of RAM. Depending on what you used your Mac for, Virtual Memory could slow down your applications (especially apps like Photoshop), but otherwise, it was cheaper than buying real RAM. Well, in Mac OS X, Virtual Memory has been replaced by an entirely new, more efficient memory scheme that operates automatically; so the Memory Control Panel, used in Mac OS 9 to turn Virtual Memory on/off, is now long gone.

8. Control Strip Is Replaced by Menu Items

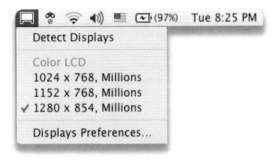

OS X: If you liked Mac OS 9's Control Strip, you'll love Mac OS X's Menu Items, which add many of the Control Strip's functions right to the menu bar. This makes your desktop less cluttered (because they're not visible in your work area), and they're always there (they don't have to be opened and closed to be used).

9. Application Folders Are Nearly Gone

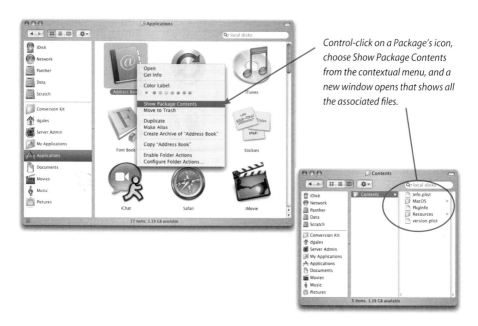

Control-click on a Package's icon, choose Show Package Contents from the contextual menu, and a new window opens that shows all the associated files.

OS X: In Mac OS 9, when you installed an application, the support files for the application (sometimes ten or more with cryptic names that disclosed nothing about their function) were typically stored along with the application in a folder. You always had the suspicion that you didn't need all of them, but you also feared that if you trashed one of them, it would be the one support file you actually needed. In Mac OS X, many applications are installed as what is called a "package." The support files are still there, but all you see on your desktop or in your Finder window is one icon. If you want to see the support files, you can Control-click on this icon and select See Package Contents from the pop-up menu. But when you want to open the application, instead of having to sift through a long list of files to find the actual application file, you just double-click on the package's icon. Another handy thing about packages is that there's now little chance of users accidentally throwing away important support files for their applications.

10. The Launcher Is Replaced by the Dock

OS X: The Launcher in Mac OS 9 let you drag your commonly used applications, folders, and files to a floating palette that gave you one-click access to them. The Launcher of old has been replaced by the Dock, which does exactly the same thing in a much more elegant way. (See Chapter One to learn how to move applications and files to the Dock for one-click launching.)

11. No SimpleSound for Recording Audio

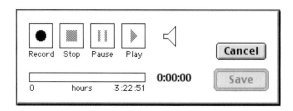

OS X: Here's one you might miss: Mac OS 9 came with an application called Simple-Sound, which let users with a built-in or external mic record audio clips that were as long as their available hard drive space would allow. So if you wanted to record your ramblings for 30 minutes, that wasn't a problem (well, your friends and family might take issue, but not the OS). In Mac OS X, the SimpleSound application is gone and hasn't been replaced. Goodbye SimpleSound, goodbye, my friend.

12. The Print Window Command Is Gone

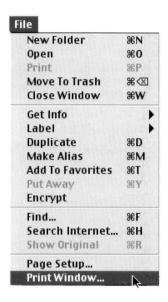

OS X: Here's another one you might miss from Mac OS 9. Back then, you could print any open Finder window by going under the File menu and choosing Print Window. If you didn't have any windows open, you could print the desktop. Sadly, this feature didn't make its way into Mac OS X, but as a workaround, you can take a screen capture of the window (Shift-Command-4-Spacebar, then click on the window), placing a PDF file on your desktop. Double-click the PDF to open in Preview, and you can print the screen capture. The problem is, a screen capture only contains what's visible on screen, so if you have a window with more content than can be shown on screen, you have to take one screen capture, scroll down, take another, and so forth. It's not pretty, it's not fun, but it works.

13. No Need to Rebuild the Desktop

OS X: In Mac OS 9, rebuilding the desktop was almost a weekly event (if you didn't rebuild it weekly, you probably should have). Well, Mac OS X itself needs no rebuilding of the desktop, so that's just one more thing you don't have to worry about. However, if you're using Mac OS X's Classic environment to run Mac OS 9-only applications (applications that haven't yet been updated to run in Mac OS X), you still have to rebuild the desktop from time to time if things in Classic mode start acting weird (icons start messing up, etc.). But luckily, if you have to rebuild the desktop in Mac OS 9, even that's easier in Mac OS X. See Chapter Nine for how to rebuild Classic's desktop.

14. No Need for Adobe Type Manager (ATM)

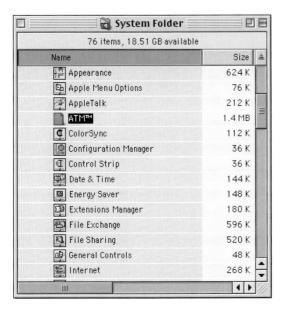

OS X: In Mac OS 9, for PostScript Type 1 fonts to look smooth on screen (especially at large point sizes), you had to have a separate Control Panel utility from Adobe called Adobe Type Manager (ATM) installed on your Mac. It was a "miracle utility" and it did an amazingly great job. As great as ATM was, Mac OS X doesn't need it because of its built-in font-smoothing technology. If you're using old applications (ones that have to run in the Classic environment because they haven't yet been updated for Mac OS X), then you still need to install ATM into your Classic system.

15. No Need to Manage Extensions

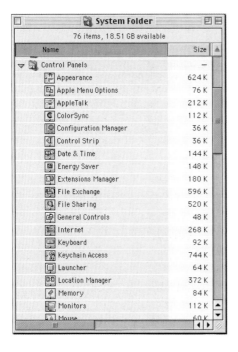

OS X: Back in Mac OS 9, you would customize your system by dropping all sorts of different Extensions and Control Panels into your System Folder. Which Extensions and Control Panels actually loaded into your system, and their loading order, was controlled by the Extensions Manager. Since you no longer drop things into your System Folder in Mac OS X, the need to manage extensions is gone, as is the Extensions Manager.

16. No More Chooser for Choosing Printers

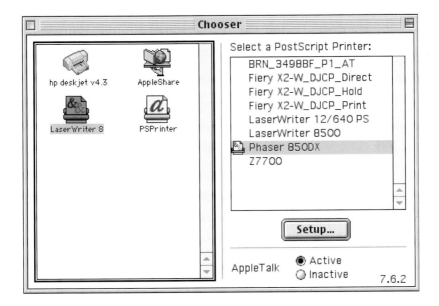

OS X: In Mac OS 9, you had to let your Mac know which printer you wanted to use by designating it in the Chooser. In Mac OS X, the Chooser is gone. Instead, you now choose your printer directly from the Print dialog of the application you're printing from, which saves untold confusion and does away with the need for a Chooser. (See Chapter Six for more on printing in Mac OS X.)

17. Finder Button View Is Replaced by Dock

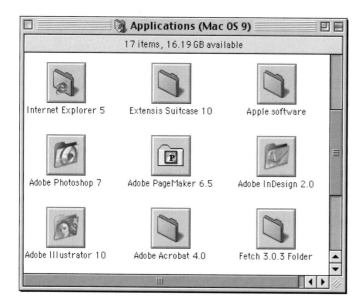

OS X: In Mac OS 9, a window mode (along with List view and Icon view), called Button view, turned your icons into large buttons for one-click access. This feature is gone in Mac OS X, as the Dock now pretty much handles one-click access to applications and files. However, some people will miss this view: People who like huge buttons. I call these people "Huge-Button-Lovers." No, it's not a very creative name, but that's all I've got. Of course, Huge-Button-Lovers can make their Mac OS X icons huge in View Options, but they'll only be huge icons, not buttons.

18. The "Sound Track" Effects Are Gone

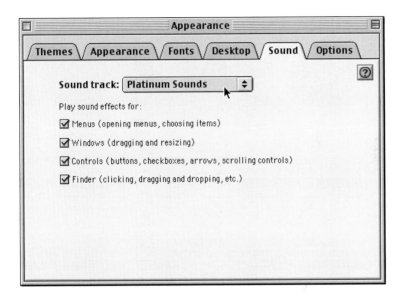

OS X: This was a mercy killing. Back in OS 9, you could have little sound effects play when you did, well…just about anything, from clicking on a menu or button to dragging a window or clicking on a file (it was in essence your operating system's "Sound Track," henceforth the name). This "sound track" was cute for about the first week, then most users scrambled to find a way to turn it off. However, the Sound Track control was buried within a tab inside the Appearance Control Panel, which was the last place most people would look (the Sound Control Panel being the first). It was Apple's hiding of the Sound Track controls that is credited by many noted historians for the severe overcrowding of asylums in the late 1990s.

19. The Application Menu Is Gone

OS X: In Mac OS 9, you switched between open applications by going to the Application menu in the upper right-hand corner of the menu bar and choosing an active application to switch to from the pop-down list. In Mac OS X, application switching is handled (like about everything else) by the Dock. You can switch to any running application by simply clicking on its icon in the Dock. An even cooler feature introduced in Panther is stepping through open applications using the keyboard shortcut Command-Tab. When you hold this key combination, all the icons for your running applications appear in the middle of your screen (as shown above). Just keep pressing the Tab key until the application that you want to switch to is highlighted. Release the keys and you're immediately switched to that app.

20. No More "Blinking" Control

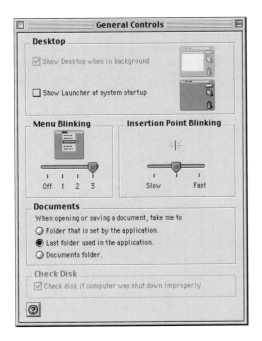

OS X: Although the term "blinking" is sometimes used when problems arise (as in "I can't get my 'blinking' iBook to start up"), the blinking in question here was found in Mac OS 9's General Controls Control Panel. This is where you could chose how many times a menu item would blink when you selected it (as you can see from the capture above, you had the choice of 1, 2, 3 or to turn the blinking off). You could also control the speed at which your I-beam text cursor blinked, from Slow to Fast. Now, in Mac OS X, you have one less thing to worry about, because Apple has decided the speed of both. Basically, you've lost control of your blinking…(you can add an additional word after blinking, if you're so inclined).

Index

informIT
www.informit.com

National Association of
Photoshop Professionals

The most powerful tool for Adobe® Photoshop®
doesn't come in the box

To get good at Photoshop, you have to think outside the box. To get really "Photoshop-guru, crazy-good," join the National Association of Photoshop Professionals (NAPP). It's the world's most complete resource for Photoshop training, education, and news. And when it comes to getting really good at Photoshop, it's the right tool for the job.

NAPP MEMBER BENEFITS INCLUDE:

- Free subscription to *Photoshop User*, the award-winning Adobe Photoshop "how-to" magazine

- Exclusive access to NAPP's private members-only Web site, loaded with tips, tutorials, downloads, and more

- Discounts on Photoshop training seminars, training videos, and books

- Free Photoshop tech support from our Help Desk and Advice Desk

- Get special member deals on everything from color printers to software upgrades to Zip disks, and everything in between

- Print and Web designers can earn professional certification and recognition through NAPP's new certification program

- Learn from the hottest Photoshop gurus in the industry at PhotoshopWorld, NAPP's annual convention

**The National Association of
Photoshop® Professionals**
The Photoshop® Authority

One-year membership is only $99 (U.S. funds)
Call 800-738-8513 (or 813-433-5000)
or enroll online at **www.photoshopuser.com**

For more info on NAPP, visit www.photoshopuser.com